Shakespeare's
Modern Collaborators

Shakespeare

Series edited by Simon Palfrey and Ewan Fernie

To Be Or Not To Be Douglas Bruster
Shakespeare Thinking Philip Davis
Shakespeare Inside Amy Scott-Douglass
Shakespeare and the Political Way Elizabeth Frazer
Godless Shakespeare Eric S. Mallin
Shakespeare's Double Helix Henry S. Turner
Shakespearean Metaphysics Michael Witmore

Lukas Erne

Shakespeare's
Modern Collaborators

continuum

Continuum
The Tower Building, 11 York Road, London SE1 7NX
80 Maiden Lane, Suite 704, New York NY 10038

www.continuumbooks.com

© Lukas Erne 2008

All rights reserved. No part of this publication may be reproduced or transmitted in any form or by any means, electronic or mechanical, including photocopying, recording, or any information storage or retrieval system, without prior permission in writing from the publishers.

Lukas Erne has asserted his right under the Copyright, Designs and Patents Act, 1988, to be identified as Author of this work.

First published 2008

British Library Cataloguing-in-Publication Data
A catalogue record for this book is available from the British Library.

ISBN: 978-0-8264-8995-1 (hardback)
      978-0-8264-8996-8 (paperback)

Library of Congress Cataloging-in-Publication Data
A catalog record for this book is available from the Library of Congress

Typeset by Kenneth Burnley, Wirral, Cheshire
Printed and bound in Great Britain by MPG Books Ltd, Bodmin, Cornwall

Contents

	Acknowledgements	vii
	General Editors' Preface	ix
	Introduction	1
1	Establishing the Text	13
2	Framing the Text	43
3	Editing Stage Action	59
4	Editing the Real *Lear*	87
	Conclusion	103
	Abbreviations	107
	Notes	111
	Index	125

Acknowledgements

This book, like a modern edition of a Shakespeare play, is the result of a collaborative effort, and I wish to thank all those on whose contributions I have been able to rely. Ewan Fernie and Simon Palfrey have provided welcome encouragement and guidance from beginning to end. David Bevington, Jeremy Ehrlich, Neil Forsyth, Tiffany Stern, and Richard Waswo have generously read and commented on the whole typescript, while Indira Ghose, M. J. Kidnie, Ruth Morse, and Margaret Tudeau-Clayton have done so on significant parts of it. I am grateful to hosts and audiences at the University of Freiburg im Breisgau, the University of Geneva, the University of Neuchâtel, and Yale University, where I was offered the possibility to present my work in progress. I have further had the opportunity to discuss many of the ideas developed here in graduate seminars taught at Geneva and Yale, and I would like to thank my students for their insights and enthusiasm. Finally, Kareen Klein has done much precious work on the typescript, Emma Depledge and Keith McDonald have provided assistance with the photoquotes and the index, while Anna Sandeman, Colleen Coalter, and Andrew Mikolajski at Continuum have helped see this book through the press.

General Editors' Preface

Shakespeare Now! represents a new form for new approaches. Whereas academic writing is far too often ascendant and detached, attesting all too clearly to years of specialist training, *Shakespeare Now!* offers a series of intellectual adventure stories: animated with fresh and often exposed thinking, with ideas still heating in the mind.

This series of 'minigraphs' will thus help to bridge two yawning gaps in current public discourse. First, the gap between scholarly thinking and a public audience: the assumption of academics that they cannot speak to anyone but their peers unless they hopelessly dumb-down their work. Second, the gap between public audience and scholarly thinking: the assumption of regular playgoers, readers, or indeed actors, that academics write about the plays at a level of abstraction or specialization that they cannot hope to understand.

But accessibility should not be mistaken for comfort or predictability. Impatience with scholarly obfuscation is usually accompanied by a basic impatience with anything but (supposed) common sense. What this effectively means is a distrust of really thinking, and a disdain for anything that might unsettle conventional assumptions, particularly through crossing or re-drafting formal, political, or theoretical boundaries. We encourage such adventure, and base our claim to a broad audience upon it.

Here, then, is where our series is innovative: no compromising of the sorts of things that can be thought; a commitment to publishing powerful, cutting-edge scholarship; *but* a conviction that these things are essentially communicable, that we can find a language that is enterprising, individual, and shareable.

To achieve this we need a form that can capture the genuine challenge and vigour of thinking. Shakespeare is intellectually exciting, and so too are the ideas and debates that thinking about his work can provoke. But published scholarship often fails to communicate much of this. It is difficult to sustain excitement over the 80–120,000 words customary for a monograph: difficult enough for the writer, and perhaps even more so for the reader. Scholarly articles have likewise become a highly formalized mode not only of publication, but also of intellectual production. The brief length of articles means that a concept can be outlined, but its implications or application can rarely be tested in detail. The decline of sustained, exploratory attention to the singularity of a play's language, occasion, or movement is one of the unfortunate results. Often 'the play' is somehow assumed, a known and given thing that is not really worth exploring. So we spend our time pursuing collateral contexts: criticism becomes a belated, historicizing footnote.

Important things have got lost. Above all, any vivid sense as to why we are bothered with these things in the first place. Why read? Why go to plays? Why are they important? How does any pleasure they give relate to any of the things we labour to say about them? In many ways, literary criticism has forgotten affective and political immediacy. It has assumed a shared experience of the plays and then averted the gaze from any such experience, or any testing of it. We want a more ductile and sensitive mode of production; one that has more chance of capturing what people are really thinking and reading about, rather than what the pre-empting imperatives of journal or respectable monograph tend to encourage.

Furthermore, there is a vast world of intellectual possibility – from the past and present – that mainstream Shakespeare criticism has all but ignored. In recent years there has been a move away from 'theory' in literary studies: an aversion to its obscure jargon and complacent self-regard; a sense that its tricks were too easily rehearsed and that the whole game has become one of diminishing returns. This has further encouraged a retreat into the supposed safety of historicism. Of course the best such work is stimulating, revelatory, and indispensable. But too often there is little trace of any struggle; little sense that the writer is coming at the subject afresh, searching for the most appropriate language or method. Alternatively, the prose is so laboured that all trace of an urgent story is quite lost.

We want to open up the sorts of thinking – and thinkers – that might help us get at what Shakespeare is doing or why Shakespeare matters. This might include psychology, cognitive science, theology, linguistics, phenomenology, metaphysics, ecology, history, political theory; it can mean other art forms such as music, sculpture, painting, dance; it can mean the critical writing itself becomes a creative act.

In sum, we want the minigraphs to recover what the Renaissance 'essay' form was originally meant to embody. It meant an 'assay' – a trial or a test of something; putting something to the proof; and doing so in a form that is not closed-off and that cannot be reduced to a system. We want to communicate intellectual activity at its most alive: when it is still exciting to the one doing it; when it is questing and open, just as Shakespeare is. Literary criticism – that is, really thinking about words in action, plays as action – can start making a much more creative and vigorous contribution to contemporary intellectual *life*.

SIMON PALFREY AND EWAN FERNIE

Introduction

It is undoubtedly true that most of the plays traditionally ascribed to Shakespeare were indeed authored by him. If I challenge in this book the view that Shakespeare is solely responsible for the play texts we read today, I do not do so because I share the views of either the so-called anti-Stratfordians, who construct conspiracy theories to suggest that someone else wrote the plays, or deconstructionists who believe that the subject can be dissolved into various contingencies. Rather, my argument is based on scholarship which has made it obvious that Shakespeare's play texts as they reach us are the result of collaboration. What this emphasis on collaboration entails is a view of Shakespeare that contradicts a Romantic understanding, or misunderstanding, of Shakespeare as a solitary genius whose original ideas found direct and perfect expression in his plays, unhampered by any material and social constraints. Rather, a well-informed view of Shakespeare needs to start with the acknowledgement that what we think of as Shakespeare's plays have been shaped by at least four different forms of collaboration.[1]

Firstly, it has become increasingly clear in the last few years that Shakespeare, like almost all his contemporary dramatists writing for the public stage, wrote a number of plays in co-authorship. It is a convenient simplification to think that Shakespeare wrote the thirty-six plays published in the First Folio in 1623, or to think that he wrote these plays plus *Pericles*. The truth, it turns out, is rather more complex. Shakespeare appears to have collaborated on *Titus Andronicus* with George Peele, on *Timon of Athens* with

Thomas Middleton, on *Pericles* with George Wilkins, and on *King Henry VIII* and *The Two Noble Kinsmen* with John Fletcher. (The Middleton material in *Macbeth* seems to be the result of later revision, not of the original composition.) In addition, there are those plays which Shakespeare wrote with collaborators who remain difficult to identify: almost certainly *The First Part of Henry VI* and *Sir Thomas More*, probably *Edward III*, and possibly *The Second Part of Henry VI*, *The Third Part of Henry VI*, and *Arden of Faversham*. In addition, there is *Cardenio*, a lost play, on which Shakespeare also seems to have collaborated with Fletcher. So much for the solid, single-authored canon. Instead of thirty-six or thirty-seven plays by Shakespeare, he may have written no more than thirty-odd plays alone and collaborated on about a dozen others with various fellow dramatists.

Secondly, Shakespeare's staged plays were the product of intense collaboration with his fellow actors. By its very nature the theatre has always been a collaborative enterprise. Once a play text had reached the playhouse, the dramatist exerted limited or no control over it, much to Hamlet's (but not necessarily Shakespeare's) regret: 'let those that play your clowns speak no more than is set down for them' (3.2.38–39). Prior to performance, the play text was subject to a process of theatrical adaptation for which the company as a whole rather than the playwright alone must have been responsible. Theatrical abridgement was a standard feature of the preparation of a Shakespeare text for performance, and there is no reason to believe that it was exclusively undertaken by Shakespeare. Long before the play text reached the playhouse, Shakespeare also collaborated with his fellow actors insofar as he wrote certain parts with specific actors in mind and must have partly tailored the parts for their future impersonators. Even the choice of dramatic subject-matter seems to have been partly collaborative, the result of the company's attempt to capitalize on the holdings of rival companies.[2]

Thirdly, Shakespeare's early modern printed playbooks took their specific form partly through the agency of Shakespeare's printers. Spelling and punctuation were considered the compositor's responsibility, as is made clear in the first published manual of hand-press printing, Joseph Moxon's *Mechanick Exercises on the Whole Art of Printing* (1683–84). This is further borne out by the rare instance of an extant manuscript that served as printer's copy: in a short sample excerpt of forty-eight lines of Harington's translation of Ariosto's *Orlando Furioso* (1591), compositors changed the punctuation on twenty-one occasions and altered the spelling of 149 words.[3] Occasionally, compositors also introduced changes which affect the meaning, and some of them did so on a surprising scale. When setting the type for *Richard II* for the First Folio, a compositor introduced no fewer than 155 such alterations, omissions, substitutions, transpositions, interpolations, as well as additions.[4] Shakespeare's early modern printed playbooks can thus rightly be regarded as collaborations between the author, who chose and ordered the words, and his compositors, who determined the spelling and the punctuation, and occasionally even changed the words.

What these three forms of collaboration still leave unaccounted for, however, is what arguably most affects our modern reading experience of Shakespeare's play – the editor's interventions. What we read as 'Shakespeare' is decisively shaped by the collaboration between Shakespeare and his modern editor. The main argument of this book is that there is a fourth group of Shakespearean collaborators in addition to his co-authors, fellow actors, and compositors, namely his editors, the people who prepare the texts we read in modern editions. Whereas the other three groups of collaborators exerted their influence in Shakespeare's own time, editors continue to do so to this day. I wish to propose that – despite recent arguments to the contrary – the editorial intervention with which Shakespeare is mediated to us is basically beneficial. It is true that editors occasionally make mistakes and have their biases. Nevertheless, all in all, their decisions and interventions have an enabling effect, allowing today's readers to engage with Shakespeare's drama with greater ease and insight.

In order to understand why modern editorial intervention is both important and beneficial, we first need to counter two mistaken views about editors and editing. The first is that the editor – like the lexicographer, according to the famous definition in Samuel Johnson's *Dictionary* – is a harmless drudge. The second is that, on the contrary, the editor is harmful. The first view implies ignorance of the impact of editorial intervention, whereas the second is related to the misguided belief that editorial intervention is best avoided or is something that we need to be saved from, that needs to be undone or 'unedited'.

The belief that the editor is a harmless drudge is informed by the misapprehension that Shakespeare's text already exists and that the editor only needs to reproduce it correctly. In fact, modern editions of Shakespeare's plays are informed by a great variety of editorial choices and decisions, that is, by acts of critical judgement (which is why editions in which editors establish their own text instead of reproducing someone else's are called 'critical editions'). By means of these acts of critical judgement, editors decide, on the macro level, what specific textual object they edit and, on the micro level, how exactly the textual object is constituted and presented.

The traditional prejudice that editors are harmless drudges meant that critics, teachers, and students used to study Shakespeare in whatever edition was most readily to hand. Today, there is much greater awareness among Shakespeareans of the impact editors have. Indeed, this is perhaps one of the most noticeable developments in Shakespeare studies in the last thirty-odd years, partly triggered by the controversy over the texts of *King Lear* to which I shall turn in the last chapter. As a result, many of today's leading Shakespeareans have become editors. This need not mean that the view of the editor as harmless drudge is now extinct. It lives on in many classrooms. It remains implicit in the institutional practices of those who believe that a PhD thesis consisting of an edition is a second-rate thesis. As R. A. Foakes put it, it is 'paradoxical that editions, which generally demand more learning, discrimination, and scholarship and have a considerably longer shelf life than most works of criticism, should have an inferior status'.[5] It is also implicit in the criticism of those who, even though they may be paying lip service to the importance of editing at one moment, still fail to acknowledge at other moments that a critical point they are making may be true for one edition of a play but not for another (see below, p. 95).

Nonetheless, the view which has become more rather than less prominent in Shakespeare studies lately and deserves a firmer refutation than that of the editor as harmless drudge is that the editor is a harmful obfuscator. As Margreta de Grazia and Peter Stallybrass have pointed out, developments in textual studies since the 1980s have led to a 'mounting resentment toward the editorial tradition'.[6] While revisionist thinking on the texts of *King Lear* allowed many to overcome an initial naivety according to which all editions were the same, it simultaneously led to a flawed belief that 'editors had been passing off an artificial Shakespeare for the real'. The result, as de Grazia and Stallybrass point out, has been a 'denigration of editing in general'.[7]

One such denigrator, for instance, argues that modern 'editions sit between the student or the scholar and the peculiar originals from which they derive and present themselves as the thing itself',[8] adding that modern editions 'tend to restrict debate rather than facilitate it'.[9] Another critic holds that editorial 'speculations are always part of "the beholder's share," and a reader who surrenders this individual activity to the institution of editing forgoes something essential to esthetic and historical experience'.[10] Both thus claim that editing disables rather than enables the reader's engagement with Shakespeare's play texts, one writing that 'Editing promises the esthetic, but delivers anesthetic',[11] the other that 'editorial assertion by emendation or other modification dulls the attitude of the potential questioner'[12] – editing as opium for the reader.

This exemplifies what has been called 'the hyperconservative "the-best-editor-is-a-dead-editor" school, which damns all editors as unacceptably intrusive'.[13] Since it eschews editing, it argues that 'The early text or texts as printed object have to become the basic focus of study'.[14] Instead of establishing 'a workable text by the diagnosis and removal of any corruption',[15] it advocates 'books leaving the textual problems intact, removing the domesticated assertions, and obliging scholars once more to read for themselves'.[16] According to this position, the only acceptable form of textual reproduction proceeds by way of photofacsimiles which 'present the authoritative texts very much as they appeared to Shakespeare's contemporaries' and 'anchors our perception of Shakespeare's text in historical evidence untrammelled with ideal projections of its meanings'.[17]

There is no denying that Randall McLeod and Michael Warren, the two scholars to whose work I have been referring, are often astute. Their position derives from profound interest in and knowledge of textual issues rather than indifference or ignorance. Nonetheless, I disagree with their view of editing and their advocacy of 'unediting' and instead share the view that 'modern readers require mediated texts'.[18] I am not convinced, in particular, that photofacsimiles (or electronic facsimiles) present the texts 'as they appeared to Shakespeare's contemporaries'. What was familiar to Shakespeare's contemporaries seems unfamiliar to us. What was modern spelling for Shakespeare's contemporaries is no longer so today. Shakespeare's original playbooks embed assumptions about performance that are distinctly early modern, not modern. In one sense, then, modern editions present the texts more nearly 'as they appeared to Shakespeare's contemporaries' than facsimiles do. Early modern quartos and folios mean differently today than they did in Shakespeare's day, which has rightly been called a powerful argument for 'a modernized, translated, rewritten "Shakespeare"',[19] for a fully edited Shakespeare, that is.

It might be responded that facsimiles have at least the advantage of faithfully reproducing the material characteristics of the original texts, but even this would be no more than partly true. All editing involves the loss of some information, including facsimiles: 'First, the paper, ink, cloth, leather, and smell of the original edition . . . and with them the sense of a former age in which all these things were new. Second, the font, the width of margin, the shape or style of the running heads, and in some cases the feel of pages indented by standing metal type or textured by ink, or characteristically marred by broken types or uneven inking.'[20] Moreover, as Stephen Orgel has pointed out, the camera is not the neutral observer it might be taken to be: 'it turns flyspecks into punctuation marks, conceals the impression made by uninked type, will not distinguish inks (so that a handwritten correction is undetectable), knows nothing of watermarks or chainlines, those essential distinguishing features of premodern paper'.[21] The *quality* of the paper also fails to be reproduced by facsimiles, even though it undeniably carries meaning, as suggested by the complaint of the Puritan pamphleteer William Prynne, in *Histrio-mastix* (1633), that Shakespeare's Folio was printed on 'farre better paper than most Octavo or Quarto Bibles' (sig. **6v).[22] Nor can facsimiles preserve the differences which existed between different copies of the same edition of early modern books, owing to the practice of stop-press correction. A facsimile edition thus 'performs, in both printed and electronic modes, its own act of idealization',[23] and the belief that it gives us access to 'the authentic Shakespeare' or at least 'the authentic Shakespeare playbook' is illusory.

If the aim of editing were the successful reproduction of all the information contained in the original, it would be impossible. Yet it is not, which is why 'The despair voiced by some writers about the very possibility of editing, a despair which has led to this theory of "unediting", seems too pessimistic'.[24] The real question is what loss of meaning on the one hand and simultaneous production of meaning on the other hand is most desirable, and of course the answer will differ depending on the editor's evaluation of the textual evidence and the edition's intended readers or users. As Brian Gibbons puts it, 'There is no avoiding edited Shakespeare: the question is only what kind of editing.'[25] If it is accepted that an edition necessarily loses some of the information contained in the original and in that sense misrepresents it, editors can undertake their task with an awareness of how not only the reproduced, but also the reinvented document signifies. One problem with the 'unediting' position is that it construes editing solely in terms of loss. Yet since editing also constitutes a possibility to mediate desirable meaning that would otherwise not be easily available to readers, it is a task which rewards all scholarly expertise and ingenuity. It is in this sense that 'the impossibility of editing and yet the inescapability of it . . . creates and explains the excitement of textual studies today'.[26]

Some of this excitement is manifest in W. B. Worthen's suggestion that we think of editions in analogy to performance: 'Each *Hamlet* on the stage uses Shakespeare's words, and much else, to fashion a new and distinctive performance; each *Hamlet* on your shelf uses Shakespeare's words, and much else, to fashion a new and distinctive performance.'[27] There are theatrical performances, and there are textual performances, and both 'materialize the work as a unique event in time and space'.[28] This proposition not only shifts the emphasis from the loss of meaning to the production of meaning, but also moves beyond the futile quest for a 'definitive' edition: 'We have come to understand that a text may no more be definitive and authentic than it may have an "onlie begetter." The text is always constructed in accord with a set of cultural values and textual assumptions, and its making and remaking are not evidence of its contamination but are, in fact, the very conditions of its being.'[29]

The uneditors whose arguments I have addressed so far object to modern editions because they fail to preserve meaning inherent in the original editions. Other uneditors object to modern editions on different grounds – not so much because modern editions lose original meaning as that they contain objectionable meaning accrued in the course of the plays' editorial history. They argue, for instance, that 'editors have tended to downplay possible instances of female authority' or that the 'Shakespearean editions that have come down to us have already been colonized'.[30] The most influential and engaging example of the latter position is Leah Marcus's *Unediting the Renaissance*. Significantly, Marcus's monograph begins with a long introduction, entitled 'The blue-eyed witch', in which the editorial treatment of Sycorax in *The Tempest* is discussed, an editorial treatment which is shown to have been informed by sexist and imperialist assumptions. The modern editor is construed by Marcus as someone who perpetuates the politically incorrect assumptions with which earlier editors had infected the play and who abuses his position of authority and power in order to advance his conservative agenda. In other words, Marcus's modern editor is someone we need to be saved from, and salvation is attained by means of 'unediting' which, as she explains, 'requires a temporary abandonment of modern editions in favor of Renaissance editions that have not gathered centuries of editorial accretion around them'.[31]

The problem with this is not that Marcus's examination of the editorial treatment of Sycorax is somehow inaccurate. It is not. I agree with her shrewd analysis but disagree with the conclusion to which it leads her. Inadequacies in modern editions call for improvements and thus for more editions, not for their 'abandonment'.

As David Bevington puts it, 'No better explanation is needed for the frequently asked question "Why another edition?" than that editors must continually and conscientiously readdress the problems of textual interpretation in terms of contemporary values and language without losing sight of what past editors can richly provide'.[32] Marcus convinces me that the traditional editorial treatment of Sycorax was marred by mistakes, but 'when editors make mistakes, as they invariably do, the solution is not to give up the enterprise but to correct those errors in subsequent editions as thoughtfully as possible'.[33] The solution is not to 'unedit' but to train ourselves to become better readers of early modern and modern editions, an endeavour to which this book seeks to make a contribution.

The main point of Chapter 1 is to illustrate the full breadth of the editors' collaboration with Shakespeare in establishing the text. Editors modernize the spelling and the punctuation, emend mistaken or doubtful readings, regularize speech headings, rearrange prose as verse or verse as prose, indent the beginning of speeches, choose a certain spatial arrangement for specific passages, and insert act and scene breaks. By doing so, they produce meanings and shape the readers' response in ways which deserve to be analysed. Chapter 2 continues this survey of forms of editorial intervention by turning to the apparatus, annotation, collation, introduction, and so on. Chapter 3 investigates an area in which modern editors make a particularly important contribution, which is in the mediation of stage action. Shakespeare's early modern playbooks, unlike Beckett's or Pinter's, have few and often imprecise stage directions, calling for a competent modern collaborator who fills in the gaps: the editor. The exact form this collaboration takes raises important questions about the nature of play-reading and of editorial mediation. In Chapter 4, finally, I focus on the variant texts of *King Lear* in order to assess how modern editorial mediation can impact a single play. More than ten scholarly editions of this play have been published in the last twenty-five years. How do these editions differ? What, as a result, do we think *King Lear* is, and how much does our answer have to do with Shakespeare, and how much with his editors? The answer I provide demonstrates the full extent of the editors' contribution to what constitutes Shakespeare's plays for modern readers. Collectively, the four chapters demonstrate how important it is to train ourselves to become better readers not just of Shakespeare but also of modern editions.

1 Establishing the Text

As Suzanne Gossett has pointed out, 'although the ordinary reader hardly notices the text or understands the decisions that go into making it, editors know that this is the heart of their work'.[34] This chapter deals with these decisions and their impact. As I wish to address a range of issues with which editors engage in the preparation of a modern edition, my ambition is not to examine any of these issues comprehensively but instead to provide a survey of some of the most important forms editorial collaboration with Shakespeare can take.

Perhaps the modern editor's most basic task is the accurate reproduction of the copy text on which subsequent, more complex editorial operations are based. Such a reproduction may be mechanical but is not therefore without its pitfalls, as evidenced by *The Guild Shakespeare* edition of 1989, in which the opening line of Hamlet's most famous soliloquy appears as 'To be or to be, that is the Question'.[35] Nonetheless, more demanding than the reproduction of the text is the subsequent modernization of its spelling. The idea of such a modernization seems to be frowned upon by some who, I suspect, may mistake the modernization of Shakespeare's *spelling* for the modernization of his *language*. An example of the latter is the *No Sweat Shakespeare* which transforms Macbeth's 'full of sound and fury' into 'full of noise and passion'. This results in a travesty; the modernization of his spelling, by contrast, is a serious scholarly task. Of course, all the major series currently on the market modernize the spelling, including Arden, New Cambridge, and Oxford, as do the Riverside, Bevington, and

Oxford *Complete Works*. So what we read in modern editions is a text written by Shakespeare as spelt by his modern editors.

Since editors are expected to be able to spell, this may seem altogether unremarkable. It is true that some features of the modernization of spelling are straightforward: 'j' instead of 'i' ('just' for 'iust'), 'y' instead of 'ie' ('lady' for 'ladie'), 'v' instead of 'u' ('even' for 'euen'), or, conversely, 'u' instead of 'v' ('up' for 'vp'), omitted final 'e's ('dumb' for 'dumbe'), or added final 'e's ('haste' for 'hast'). Yet other modernizations involve complex editorial decisions with significant repercussions. Two questions can be highlighted here: How thoroughly should editors modernize? And what should they do when a word can be modernized in more than one way?

Concerning the first question, the Riverside and the Oxford *Complete Works* have adopted policies that are diametrically opposed, the Riverside opting for reluctant and the Oxford *Complete Works* for rigorous modernization. In the Riverside edition, 'an attempt has been made to preserve a selection of Elizabethan spelling forms that reflect, or may reflect, a distinctive contemporary pronunciation'.[36] The text therefore retains a great many spellings that are today archaic, such as 'fift' (fifth'), 'wrack' (wreck), 'vild' (vile), or 'bankrout' (bankrupt). Stanley Wells, general editor of the Oxford *Complete Works*, has objected to this practice on the grounds that 'The preservation of "a selection of Elizabethan spelling forms" has the practical disadvantage of creating a need for many more glosses than normal in a modern-spelling edition, most of them serving no purpose beyond a reassurance that the unfamiliar spelling in the text is not a misprint. . . . The policy also leads to eccentricity and the kind of obscurity that defeats the end of modernization'.[37] David Bevington, another general editor of Shakespeare's works, agrees with Wells and adds that 'rigorous modernization of spelling' leads to 'a text that is as available and contemporary as possible'.[38] The aim of the Riverside edition is instead to provide a text which suggests 'the kind of linguistic climate in which [Shakespeare] wrote'.[39] Independently of the practical disadvantages of the solution adopted in the Riverside edition, it is easy to see how the Shakespeare it implicitly constructs is vastly different from the one in Bevington and the Oxford *Complete Works*. Whereas the one easily travels across centuries to become our contemporary, the other wrote four centuries ago and was a contemporary of Edmund Spenser.

A second complex issue is how to modernize words when there are several possibilities. In early modern English, spelling was still in its pre-regulative phase, which means that a word could be spelt in different ways and that identical spellings frequently existed for words whose meaning is distinct. For instance, in *The Merchant of Venice*, Shylock says about Antonio that 'hee was wont to lende money for a Christian cursie' (Q1, E2v, 3.1.45–46), the last word being spelt 'curtsie' in the Second Quarto and the First Folio. In these and other variant spellings such as 'courtesie', the word could have either the general sense of modern 'courtesy' or mean more specifically what is now spelt 'curtsy', and each solution has been adopted in modern editions. Editors similarly need to choose in *Macbeth* when modernizing the First Witch's invitation to her fellow sisters to 'performe your Antique round' (TLN 1677, 4.1.130)[40] where the adjective can mean either antic or antique. The standard solution in modern editions is to modernize 'antic round', which is glossed as a 'grotesque dance in a circle' in the Riverside edition, but Bevington is surely right in pointing out that 'the sense of an ancient ritual is invitingly present'.[41] Similarly, the second word in Macbeth's 'Ere humane Statute purg'd the gentle Weale' (TLN 1348, 3.4.77) was an acceptable spelling of modern 'humane' and 'human'. Since neither sense is indisputably dominant here, an editor has to take a decision by modernizing the word as the one or the other.

When modernizing the spelling, editors thus may have to choose between words which in modern English are quite distinct, including 'loose' or 'lose', 'then' or 'than', 'born' or 'borne', 'travel' or 'travail', 'lest' or 'least', and 'of' or 'off'.[42] This obligation to choose has been adduced as an argument against modernizing the spelling on the grounds that the modern editor's adoption of the one or the other word constitutes a loss of meaning if the early modern spelling could mean both.[43] However, as has rightly been pointed out, 'even the preservation of Folio or Quarto spellings cannot solve the problem, for modern readers have in effect internalized the modernizing process that the editor performs on the text'.[44] In other words, what an editor cannot restore is the early modern readers' capacity to be attuned to the multiple forms a word could take: 'humane', to modern readers, means 'humane', not 'human', or 'human and/or humane', as it may have to early modern readers. The best a modern editor can therefore do is choose the meaning that seems dominant and explain the other meaning in the annotation.

Few editors seem aware of such an alternative meaning in the following passage (I quote from Bevington):

GONZALO This Tunis, sir, was Carthage.
ADRIAN Carthage?
GONZALO I assure you, Carthage.
ANTONIO His word is more than the miraculous harp.
SEBASTIAN He hath raised the wall, and houses too.
ANTONIO What impossible matter will he make easy next?
SEBASTIAN I think he will carry this island home in his pocket and give it his son for an apple.
ANTONIO And, sowing the kernels of it in the sea, bring forth more islands.
GONZALO Ay.
ANTONIO Why, in good time.

(*The Tempest*, 2.1.85–97)

Gonzalo's 'Ay' renders in modernized spelling the First Folio's 'I' (TLN 766), and the Riverside edition plausibly glosses the word as 'a sarcastic expression of approbation'. It seems equally possible, however, that Gonzalo is starting a sentence with the first person pronoun but is immediately interrupted by Antonio.[45] If so, Antonio's self-serving rudeness would seem very much in character, depriving honest Gonzalo of speech as he had earlier deprived Prospero of his dukedom. As the present example suggests, editorial decisions in modernizing the spelling can easily affect characterization.

A famous example that corroborates this point is the epithet used for the three witches in *Macbeth*. In modern editions, they are the 'weird sisters', but the First Folio in fact calls them 'weyward' and 'weyard'. By modernizing the spelling to 'weird', modern editors are partly influence by Holinshed, who calls them 'weird' in Shakespeare's source, but are also guided by the *Oxford English Dictionary* (OED), which records 'weyward' as an early modern spelling of 'weird'. Yet the only witness the OED adduces for this spelling is *Macbeth*, and the authority on which the identity of 'weyward' and 'weird' is argued is Lewis Theobald's eighteenth-century edition of *Macbeth*.[46] If we add to this circular reasoning that 'weyward' is an early modern spelling variant of 'wayward' attested outside Shakespeare, we realize that the witches' epithet could be modernized as either 'weird' or 'wayward' and that early modern readers may well have registered both meanings. The ambivalence surely matters: 'weird' associates the sisters with prophecy (via the Old English 'wyrd' = fate), whereas 'wayward' suggests 'perversion and vagrancy'.[47] A central question *Macbeth* raises is that of the witches' agency: do they foretell or create evil? The latter arguably exculpates Macbeth; the former does not. The question is thus intimately related to how editors modernize the spelling.

In addition to the spelling, modern editors need to decide on the punctuation. The rules governing early modern punctuation are still imperfectly understood, but it seems clear that, contrary to modern punctuation, which is chiefly grammatical and logical, early modern punctuation was strongly rhetorical. Commas, semi-colons, colons, and periods can thus represent pauses of increasing length.[48] As a result, early modern practice is so different from modern practice that 'the punctuation of the control-text would often bewilder or mislead a modern reader, and must be altered in a modern-spelling edition'.[49] The modernization of punctuation seems all the more desirable as the early quartos and folios, despite occasional arguments to the contrary, do not give us access to Shakespeare's punctuation, as ample evidence bears out.[50] This does not mean that the early modern playbooks may be disregarded; on the contrary, 'intelligent respect must be paid to the punctuation of original texts',[51] and editors should be open to the possibility that early modern 'punctuational choices' can constitute 'a revealing adjunct to critical interpretations and performance of the texts'.[52] Nevertheless, modern editors usefully collaborate with Shakespeare by modernizing the punctuation with an aim 'to interpret as clearly as possible in modern terms the seeming intent of the original'.[53]

Since this intent is not always easily recovered, editors face tough choices.[54] When Cleopatra asks Alexas, 'What was he sad, or merry?' (TLN 581, 1.5.53), we may modernize as 'What, was he sad or merry?' or 'What was he, sad or merry?' Caesar's 'Looke you sad Friends' (TLN 3140, 5.1.26) later in the same play similarly allows for two possibilities: 'Look you sad, friends?' or 'Look you, sad friends, . . .'. A slightly more complex case is the opening of Sonnet 84 which reads in the Quarto of 1609: 'Who is it that sayes most, which can say more, / Then this rich praise, that you alone, are you'. Does the first line initiate two syntactically parallel questions (Who is it that says most? Which can say more?), or a meaning paraphrased by Stephen Booth as 'Who is it among those that say most who can say more than this?' Arden 3 opts for the first interpretation: 'Who is it that says most? Which can say more, / Than this rich praise: that you alone are you.' New Penguin, by contrast, encourages the second reading: 'Who is it that says most which can say more / Than this rich praise – that you alone are you.' The Oxford edition arguably leaves open both possibilities by preserving the Quarto's comma after 'most': 'Who is it that says most, which can say more / Than this rich praise: that you alone are you.'

A special kind of problem can present itself when more than one substantive text of a play is extant. In the opening scene of *Hamlet*, Marcellus's 'Therefore I have entreated him along / With us to watch the minutes of this night' (1.1.30–31) makes it possible for an editor to choose between different solutions in the early editions. The Second Quarto connects 'With us' with 'to watch' by inserting a comma after 'along', whereas the First Folio links the same words with 'along' by having a comma after 'us'. Editors can thus decide to follow the punctuation in their copy text (as Riverside does), or they can omit both commas (like Bevington) and thus allow for either reading.

The Second Quarto and First Folio similarly disagree on the punctuation in one of Hamlet's famous speeches, and the editor's decision of how to punctuate has important repercussions on what sense readers make of the speech. Here are the two versions in Q2 and F1:

What peece of worke is a man, how noble in reason, how infinit in faculties, in forme and moouing, how expresse and admirable in action, how like an Angell in apprehension, how like a God
(Q2, F2r)

What a piece of worke is man! how Noble in Reason? how infinite in faculty? in forme and mouing how expresse and admirable? in Action, how like an Angel? in apprehension how like a God?
(F1, TLN 1350–53)

The Folio's exclamation and question marks are in striking contrast with Q2's commas, and Dover Wilson argued that Q2 conveyed 'the brooding Ham[let]'[55] as opposed to the more outward, declamatory character in the F1. Yet the most important difference between Q2 and F1 does not reside in question marks and commas but in the way the words are grouped. In F1, the speech has a regular pattern, with five consecutive 'how . . . in' or 'in . . . how' constructions. In Q2, by contrast, this pattern is interrupted when the speech reaches the climactic 'how like a God'. F1's Hamlet calls man infinite not only in faculties but also in form and motion ('moouing'). Q2's Hamlet, by contrast, says that man's form and motion are well-modelled ('expresse') and admirable. In F1, Hamlet's attribute of angels is apprehension; in Q2, it is action. There is little agreement among modern editors as to which reading is preferable. Bevington and Arden 2, for instance, prefer F1's, whereas Riverside and Arden 3 opt for Q2's. Here and elsewhere, modern editors decisively shape Shakespeare's play texts by deciding how to punctuate them.

Perhaps the most obvious way in which modern editors collaborate with Shakespeare is through emendation – that is, by means of alteration designed to correct or improve the original text. As Gary Taylor writes in an essay significantly entitled 'Inventing Shakespeare', 'Every time an editor emends a text he is, to an extent, reconstructing its author in his own image'.[56] Since every Shakespeare play has been perceived to need emendation in a number of passages, every modern editor can be said to be participating in this authorial reconstruction.

There are various reasons why editors may consider emendation necessary.[57] Most common are passages thought to make imperfect or no sense as a result of corruption in the text's transmission. Alternatively, the textual problem may originate with Shakespeare. When 'Don Peter' is mentioned twice at the beginning of *Much Ado about Nothing*, but the character is called 'Don Pedro' throughout the rest of the play, it seems plausible to assume that Shakespeare changed his mind, and editors emend the name accordingly. Another reason for emendation is a passage that poses problems in terms of the staging, for instance because a character who speaks has not been provided with an entrance. Also, editors occasionally emend in order to regularize the metre. When Romeo enumerates the guests invited to the Capulets' feast, modern editions read 'My fair niece Rosaline, and Livia', even though Q2 and all seventeenth-century editions that ultimately derive from it omit the conjunction. Since one of Shakespeare's distinctive features as a dramatic poet is that his metrical practice was extremely varied, this form of emendation seems particularly hazardous, though, and modern editors rightly practise it with greater reluctance than their eighteenth-century predecessors did. Alexander Pope, for instance, 'emended' Friar Laurence's 'Reuolts from true birth, stumbling on abuse' (Q2, E1r, 2.3.20) to the metrically more regular 'Revolts to vice and stumbles on abuse', although it seems clear to most editors today that the line in Q2 appropriately stumbles.

When textual corruption of some kind seems beyond dispute, the exact form emendation should take can be far from clear. When Mercutio says 'We waste our lights in vaine, lights lights by day' (Q2, C1v, 1.4.45), there is clearly something wrong with the end of the line, but should it be emended to 'like lights' (New Cambridge, Oxford *Complete Works*, Riverside), 'light lights' (Arden 2, Oxford), or 'like lamps' (New Penguin, Bevington)? Similarly, when the beginning of line 2 in Sonnet 146 repeats the words of the end of line 1, editors agree that emendation is necessary:

> Poore soule the center of my sinfull earth,
> My sinfull earth these rebel powers that thee array,

Yet how are the first three words of line 2 best emended? By 'Feeding' (Arden 3), 'Spoiled by' (Oxford), or 'Thrall to' (Bevington)? Or by one of the solutions mentioned in the New Cambridge edition: 'Fooled by', 'Starved by', 'Foiled by', 'Pressed by', 'Rebuke', 'Bearing', 'Fenced by', or 'Gulled by'? Or by one of the more than eighty (!) other readings that have been proposed?[58] It makes little sense to argue that one of these readings is correct and the others wrong, yet an editor's choice can have definite critical implications. Helen Vendler, for instance, has offered a close reading of the sonnet which relies importantly on the emendation – 'Feeding' – which she defends.[59]

While an important editorial task is how to emend, it is no less important, in other cases, to decide whether to emend. Eighteenth-century editors confidently tried to improve on the early texts, but modern editors do so more reluctantly. Clearly, it is hard to draw the line between what is and what is not desirable emendation, between legitimately fixing the text when it is broken and meddling with it in ways which seem unnecessary or downright harmful.[60] For instance, the first word in Juliet's 'runnawayes eyes may wincke' (Q2, G1v, 3.2.6) was long supposed to be corrupt, and more than forty emendations have been proposed (New Cambridge). Yet recent editions accept the Q2 reading and simply modernize its spelling to 'runaways' eyes may wink'. Likewise, on arriving in the Forest of Arden, Rosalind's first words are 'O *Iupiter*, how merry are my spirits' (*As You Like It*, TLN 784, 2.3.1), which editors long emended to 'weary are my spirits', though the New Cambridge edition has recently restored the Folio reading, arguing that Rosalind is 'rejoicing in adversity – or being ironic'. Even what has been considered one of the triumphs of eighteenth-century Shakespeare editing has recently come under forceful attack. Reporting the death of Falstaff, Mistress Quickly says in *Henry V* that 'his Nose was as sharpe as a Pen, and a Table of greene fields' (TLN 838–39), which Lewis Theobald, in 1733, famously emended to 'and 'a [he] babbled of green fields' (2.3.16–17). Duncan Salkeld has argued, however, that the words are referring to the 'quadrants (sometimes today called "fields")' on a backgammon board which were 'marked with six sharp, triangular "points"', concluding that 'the Folio makes disarmingly simple sense when understood as referring to the design on a backgammon board'.[61] It may well be that a twenty-first-century edition will restore the Folio reading. Thanks to the sustained attention by scholars and editors to individual passages, Shakespeare's texts keep changing in subtle and important ways.

Since emendation requires both scholarship and creativity, it is perhaps not surprising that attitudes towards it have considerably differed. W. W. Greg wrote about it in almost mystic terms: 'At its finest, it is an inspiration, a stirring of the spirit, which obeys no laws and cannot be produced to order'.[62] Fredson Bowers's view was far more sober: 'just about every emendation has been proposed that is likely to be adopted, and editing has largely resolved itself to the exercise of personal choice among the known alternatives'.[63] This recalls Samuel Johnson's scepticism, unusual for an eighteenth-century editor: 'As I practiced conjecture more, I learned to trust it less; and after I had printed a few plays, resolved to insert none of my own readings in the text.'[64] Recently, however, the editors of the Oxford *Complete Works* have adopted a very different attitude, and Gary Taylor has explicitly advocated a creative approach, preferring 'mimetic' to 'anonymous' emendation: 'it is of course better to insert something neutral than something uncharacteristic; but if you *can* find something unmistakably characteristic to fill the gap, that is even better'.[65] An example of Taylor's creative approach to emendation is his edition of *Pericles* in the Oxford *Complete Works*, which contains a number of passages rewritten by the editor with the help of the novella *The Painfull Adventures of Pericles Prince of Tyre*, by Shakespeare's collaborator George Wilkins. The case has led to understandable complaints that 'Taylor refashioned himself as a co-author'.⁶⁶ On the other hand, it may simply be an extreme example of the contention of this book that modern editors should be considered Shakespeare's collaborators.

In the case of emendation, editors adopt readings on the basis of what they think Shakespeare wrote, or would have written, if he had carefully revised his text. Yet in the following – most unusual – case, editors have to decide based not simply on what they think Shakespeare scripted but on what they believe the compositors set. In *The Tempest*, following the masque, Ferdinand exclaims:

> Let me live here ever!
> So rare a wondered father and a wise
> Makes this place Paradise.
> (4.1.122–24)

So the passage reads in most twentieth-century editions, including Frank Kermode's Arden 2 of 1954, until Jeanne Addison Roberts argued in 1978 that what looks like a long 's' in the Folio is in fact a broken 'f' ('"Wife" or "Wise"').⁶⁷ She maintained that the crossbar of the 'f' broke early in the print run, but that two copies of the First Folio in the Folger Shakespeare Library still show the letter intact. This news came as comfort to some: after all, 'wise' implies that, surprisingly, Ferdinand's paradise includes Prospero but not Miranda; 'wife', by contrast, restores Miranda to the text and suggests a paradise that is more in line with Milton's. The new reading clearly had important ideological implications, Stephen Orgel proclaiming that 'wife' 'is a reading whose time has come'.⁶⁸ He adopted it in his Oxford edition, as did several other editions, including New Cambridge and Folger. Yet in the meantime, Peter W. M. Blayney returned to the First Folio, looking at each of the many copies in the Folger's extensive collection. Aided by a lens with 'magnification to the 200th power', he concluded that the letter is an 's' in all instances and that those Roberts identified with 'f' were the result of 'blotted ink, not a broken crossbar'.[69] As a result, the Arden 3 edition (1999) has returned to 'wise', as has the 5th edition of Bevington's *Complete Works* (2003), though the updated 4th edition of 1997 still reads 'wife'. While most editions have thus been following the tides of bibliographical scholarship, the editors of the Oxford *Complete Works* (published after Roberts but before Blayney) found 'wise' the 'more convincing reading',[70] arguing that the two words may have been confused when the text was set. Editors will have to go on choosing between 'wife' and 'wise', and their choice will have important critical repercussions and ideological implications.[71]

A matter on which editors can spend a considerable amount of time without most readers being aware of the choices that have gone into the establishment of the text is lineation. When Shakespeare writes in verse, the early playbooks usually have a succession of lines with the same or a similar metrical pattern, usually iambic pentameter. But there are numerous passages with short or long lines that do not conform to this pattern. In these cases, editors may opt to relineate the verse if the resulting arrangement seems metrically an improvement and more in line with Shakespeare's habitual practice. Folio *Macbeth* contains the following passage:

> This supernaturall solliciting
> Cannot be ill; cannot be good.
> If ill? why hath it giuen me earnest of successe,
> (TLN 241–43)

A pentameter is followed by a tetrameter and a hexameter. We know that Shakespeare occasionally used tetrameters and hexameters, even amidst blank verse. Nevertheless, the passage can easily be rearranged so as to consist of three iambic pentameters, which is why almost all editions relineate as follows:

> This supernatural soliciting
> Cannot be ill, cannot be good. If ill,
> Why hath it given me earnest of success
> (1.3.131–33)

However, Kenneth Muir, in Arden 2, announced in the introduction that his text would be 'closer to that of the First Folio than any since the seventeenth century, especially with regard to lineation',[72] and printed

> This supernatural soliciting
> Cannot be ill;-cannot be good:–
> If ill, why hath it given me earnest of success,
> (1.3.130–32)

Muir argued that 'Shakespeare's irregularities were deliberate', though he granted that 'it is not always possible to distinguish between such irregularities and those for which transcriber or printer is responsible'.[73] Refusing to relineate, Muir thus considers the passage a deliberate Shakespearean irregularity, whereas other editors implicitly assume that Shakespeare's verse in this passage is regular and that irregularity was introduced through other agency. What is at stake, quite clearly, is a judgement on how metrically regular or irregular Shakespeare is, a judgement which is embedded in modern editions in the way editors relineate or refuse to do so. Is Shakespeare's verse more like Donne's or more like Pope's? To a certain extent, the answer we give to such a question depends on the people who decide, in effect, how Shakespeare's verse works: his modern editors.

In determining which passages should be arranged into iambic pentameters, a particular problem editors face are so-called shared lines. Act 2 Scene 3 in *Macbeth* begins with the Porter's prose, but after his exit and Macbeth's entrance, modern editions arrange the lines as follows:

LENNOX	Good morrow, noble sir.
MACBETH	Good morrow, both.
MACDUFF	Is the King stirring, worthy thane?
MACBETH	Not yet.

(2.3.43–44)

Macbeth's dimeter and monometer respond to and complete Lennox's trimeter and Macduff's tetrameter. In terms of content and metre, the short speeches seem to complement each other, amounting to iambic pentameters. The First Folio arranges these speeches differently, however:

Lenox. Good morrow, Noble Sir.
Macb. Good morrow both.
Macd. Is the King stirring, worthy *Thane*?
Macb. Not yet.

(TLN 787–90)

On a purely visual level, this arrangement suggests four lines of prose; by indenting the second part of the verse lines, editors decide instead that the passage consists of two lines of verse. Indentation to suggest shared lines is a practice that was not adopted until 1768, by Edward Capell, and it did not become a standard feature until George Steevens's variorum edition of 1793.[74] The line formatting used by Capell, Steevens, and modern editors in their wake has the considerable merit of making visible the metrical structure of divided lines. It also allows for line numbering of Shakespeare's verses as wholes, rather than of the mechanically printed lines.[75] However, Paul Bertram, in 1980, argued against the editorially produced 'white spaces in Shakespeare' between speech heading and indented speech.[76] Reminding us of the arrangement of such passages in pre-eighteenth-century editions and maintaining that the practice modern editors have inherited reflects eighteenth-century ideas of scansion, Bertram encouraged editors to follow the line formatting of the earliest playbooks. Bertram's argument prompted a thoughtful response by Paul Werstine: 'To accept Bertram's argument that metrically linked speeches reflect eighteenth-century practice, not Shakespeare's, one must ignore the example of Ben Jonson and dismiss as lucky accidents the hundreds of cases in the early printed texts of Shakespeare's plays in which successive short lines can be linked together to form perfect pentameters. Ben Jonson almost invariably insisted that his printers set short speeches that together form complete pentameters all on the same line.'[77]

As a result of this scholarly debate, the modern editors' responsibility in lineating Shakespeare's verse has been reaffirmed, raising the question of how far this responsibility should extend. In the above-quoted passage from Act 2, Scene 3 in *Macbeth*, shared lines result in metrical regularity and semantic complementarity, but many other passages are less clear-cut. Bevington has argued that even though 'Shakespeare clearly conceived many such short lines as linked together into verse (usually iambic pentameter)', editors 'are too willing to link short lines when the case for linkage is metrically unconvincing',[78] adding elsewhere that editorially created verse lines 'can vary from three to six or seven feet and can introduce other irregularities that we would find extraordinary if found in a regular verse line in the original'.[79] Here is the end of a speech by Macbeth followed by the beginning of one by Banquo as lineated in the First Folio:

> Our will became the seruant to defect,
> Which else should free haue wrought.
>   *Banq.* All's well
> I dreamt last Night of the three weyward Sisters:
>   (TLN 593–96)

The last line of Macbeth's speech is a trimeter and the first line of Banquo's a monometer which, if joined, result in a tetrameter, not a pentameter. Some modern editions (New Cambridge, New Penguin, Oxford, Oxford *Complete Works*, Riverside) nonetheless print them as a shared line but others (Bevington, Folger) do not. The decision affects how we think not only of Shakespeare's metrical practice but also of how the speeches are related, a transitional shared line emphasizing the continuity between them and two separate lines insisting on their independence. Here and elsewhere, editorial lineation subtly shapes the way we read Shakespeare's dramatic language.

If one decision editors have to take is how to lineate verse, another is whether to print certain passages as verse at all or to arrange them as prose instead. The early quarto and folio editions do not always provide reliable guidance. The First Quarto of *King Lear*, for instance, repeatedly has prose where the First Folio and modern editions have verse. Prose/verse confusion may reflect non-authorial agency of various kinds. For example, when compositors had to print a predetermined amount of text on a page, they sometimes had to waste or save space and did so by printing prose as verse or verse as prose. On other occasions, compositors with an insufficient provision of capital letters with which verse lines begin printed verse as prose.

If a speech originally printed as prose conforms to straightforward blank verse, modern editors will lose little sleep over it, but other passages pose greater difficulty. It seems repeatedly unclear, for instance, whether the Nurse in *Romeo and Juliet* speaks verse or prose. In Act 1, Scene 3, the Second Quarto, on which modern editions are based, prints the Nurse's part in prose which modern editions, following various eighteenth-century editors, arrange as verse. In Act 1, Scene 5, the Nurse in Q2 speaks verse which modern editors print as such. In Act 2, Scene 3, she reverts to prose in Q2. Late in the scene, when Mercutio and Benvolio have left, the conversation between the Nurse and Romeo turns to the subject of Juliet. At this point, Q2 prints Romeo's speeches as verse, which leads modern editors to rearrange some of the Nurse's prose speeches as verse. Yet they disagree on individual speeches, like the following, quoted from the Oxford edition:

> Well, sir, my mistress is the sweetest lady.
> Lord, lord, when 'twas a little, prating thing–
> O there is a nobleman in town, one Paris,
> That would fain lay knife aboard; but she, good soul,
> Had as lief see a toad, a very toad,
> As see him. I anger her sometimes,
> And tell her that Paris is the properer man;
> But I'll warrant you, when I say so she looks
> As pale as any clout in the versal world.
> Does not 'rosemary' and 'Romeo' begin
> Both with a letter?
>
> (2.3.186–96)

Is this prose (despite the intermittent verse rhythm) or verse (despite the irregularity)? Arden 2, New Penguin, Bevington, and Riverside decide it is prose, whereas Jill Levenson's Oxford edition and the Oxford *Complete Works* opt for verse. Before we claim that the matter is of no consequence, we would do well to ask, with Stephen Orgel, 'What is involved in deciding that such examples are "really" not verse but prose, or not prose but verse?'[80] As Orgel points out, the assumptions are likely not to be 'merely metrical' but have to do 'with decisions about how we want the particular character to be perceived'.[81] In the case of the Nurse, the hesitation between prose and verse can alert us to her liminal status in the play: do we think of her chiefly as a comic character and a 'mere' wet-nurse (for whom prose seems appropriate), or do we consider her as an important agent involved in the play's tragic intrigue (who deserves the distinction of verse)? Editorial choice of prose or verse can be intimately related to characterization.

Decisions about verse and prose concern all parts of the dramatic text, but occasionally there are more local decisions to be taken which affect the spatial arrangement of a limited amount of text, typically a song, a poem, or a letter. For instance, how exactly editors edit the letter to Malvolio (*Twelfth Night*, 2.5) is a matter of some consequence, as a recent essay by Patricia Parker shows.[82] Similarly, a decision any editor of *Romeo and Juliet* has to face is that of the layout of the dialogue of the first encounter of Romeo and Juliet at the Capulets' feast (I.5). What many people remember about this passage is that Romeo and Juliet share a sonnet when they first speak to each other. While this is not wrong, it is not the full truth either. In fact, we think Romeo and Juliet share a sonnet because that is what some modern editions suggest through annotation and layout. Here, for example, is how the passage appears in the Oxford *Complete Works*:

> ROMEO (*to Juliet, touching her hand*)
>   If I profane with my unworthiest hand
>   This holy shrine, the gentler sin is this:
>   My lips, two blushing pilgrims, ready stand
>   To smooth that rough touch with a tender kiss.   95
> JULIET
>   Good pilgrim, you do wrong your hand too much,
>   Which mannerly devotion shows in this.
>   For saints have hands that pilgrims' hands do touch,
>   And palm to palm is holy palmers' kiss.
> ROMEO
>   Have not saints lips, and holy palmers, too?   100
> JULIET
>   Ay, pilgrim, lips that they must use in prayer.
> ROMEO
>   O then, dear saint, let lips do what hands do:
>   They pray; grant thou, lest faith turn to despair.
> JULIET
>   Saints do not move, though grant for prayers' sake.
> ROMEO
>   Then move not while my prayer's effect I take.   105
>   *He kisses her*

The layout serves to highlight the shared sonnet by means of indentation of lines two, four, six, eight, ten, and twelve. Here, by contrast, is how the same passage appears in the First and Second Quartos:

> *Rom:* If I prophane with my vnworthie hand,
> This holie shrine, the gentle sinne is this:
> My lips two blushing Pilgrims ready stand,
> To smooth the rough touch with a gentle kisse.
> *Iuli:* Good Pilgrime you doe wrong your hand, too
> Which mannerly deuotion shewes in this: (much,
> For Saints haue hands which holy Palmers tou'ch,
> And Palme to Palme is holy Palmers kisse.
> *Rom:* Haue not Saints lips, and holy Palmers too?
> *Iuli:* Yes Pilgrime lips that they must vse in praier.
> *Ro:* Why then faire saint, let lips do what hands doo,
> They pray, yeeld thou, least faith turne to dispaire.
> *Iu:* Saints doe not mooue though: grant nor praier
>   forsake.
> *Ro:* Then mooue not till my praiers effect I take.

> *Ro.* If I prophane with my vnworthiest hand,
> This holy shrine, the gentle sin is this,
> My lips two blushing Pylgrims did readie stand,
> To smoothe that rough touch with a tender kis.
> *Iu.* Good Pilgrim you do wrōg your hād too much
> Which mannerly deuocion showes in this,
> For saints haue hands, that Pilgrims hands do tuch,
> And palme to palme is holy Palmers kis.
> *Ro.* Haue not Saints lips and holy Palmers too?
> *Iuli.* I Pilgrim, lips that they must vse in praire.
> *Rom.* O then deare Saint, let lips do what hands do,
> They pray (grant thou) least faith turnes to dispaire.
> *Iu.* Saints do not moue, thogh grant for praiers sake.
> *Ro.* Then moue not while my praiers effect I take.

In the early modern editions, typography suggests dramatic continuity rather than a poetic set piece that stands apart from the rest.

What complicates matters is that rhymed verse in this passage is in fact not confined to the first fourteen lines of dialogue between Romeo and Juliet. Tybalt's four lines immediately preceding the lovers' dialogue form two couplets and, more importantly, Romeo and Juliet's fourteen-line sonnet is followed by another quatrain with the rhyme scheme *abab*. In fact, it might be argued that Romeo and Juliet do not simply share a sonnet, or at least not in the narrow sense to which the use of the term has been restricted since the eighteenth century (see *OED*, sonnet), but that they share an eighteen-line passage with three quatrains and a couplet. If we want to argue that the dialogue between Romeo and Juliet consists of one poem, we would have to call it not simply a 'sonnet' but rather a 'caudate sonnet' (from the Italian 'sonnetto caudato'), meaning a 'tailed sonnet', consisting of a standard sonnet followed by a coda. The form seems to have been invented by the Italian poet Francesco Berni (1497–1536).[83] Examples in early modern England are rare, though John Milton's 'On the New Forcers of Conscience Under the Long Parliament', a fourteen-line sonnet followed by two tails of a half line and a couplet each, is a notable exception.

Another interpretation of Romeo and Juliet's final quatrain is possible, though: it is a commonplace in criticism of *Romeo and Juliet* that Shakespeare dramatizes the various encounters between the two lovers in a way that announces their tragic deaths long before they actually happen. At the end of the 'Balcony Scene', Juliet ominously tells Romeo that 'I should kill thee with much cherishing' (2.2.184); the 'Betrothal Scene' is riddled with anticipatory words such as 'sorrow', 'death', 'violent ends', 'die' (2.6.2–10); and when the two lovers last talk, Juliet's 'ill-divining soul' already sees Romeo 'As one dead in the bottom of a tomb' (3.5.54–56). Their first encounter is usually considered the one exception to this pattern, the one moment in which the intensity of their love is not overshadowed by premonitions of their deaths. It seems possible to argue, however, that Romeo and Juliet start a second shared sonnet that gets cut off as the Nurse interrupts them, doing to the lovers' sonnet what the play ends up doing to their lives.

Inevitably, editors of *Romeo and Juliet* have to choose between various spatial arrangements of the verse in this passage, and just as inevitably that spatial arrangement carries meaning, encouraging a certain interpretation over another. Some editions (including Arden 2, Bevington, and Riverside) prefer the dramatic continuity suggested by the spatial arrangement of the early quartos which does not draw attention to the pattern of the rhyming verse. This spatial arrangement refrains from privileging the young lovers at the expense of the other characters, clearly a defensible choice. Alternatively, an editor can typographically highlight the sonnet, or the sonnet and the following quatrain. Such a typographic arrangement may encourage the interpretation that Romeo and Juliet share a sonnet and feel so at home in the lyric form of Petrarchan love that they immediately start a second sonnet only to be cut off by the Nurse who, in such a reading, turns out to be the first of a series of external forces thwarting their love. In this case, the decision not to preserve the spatial arrangement of the copy-text turns out to be not a loss of meaning that an editor would deem worthy to preserve but a way of editorially mediating to the reader meaning which the original document does not make as easily available.

Whereas special layout to signal rhyme is relatively rare in modern editions, act and scene division is a standard feature. Despite what we might think, the division often does not depend on objective criteria which have long led to uniform practice but instead are a result of how modern editors decide to carve up the plays. What partly accounts for the difficulty modern editors face is that none of Shakespeare's playbooks published during his lifetime contained any act and scene divisions. Q1 *Othello* (1622) is the first to note breaks, at the beginning of acts 2 ('*Actus*. 2. / Scœna I.', D2v), 4 ('*Actus*. 4.', I4r), and 5 ('*Actus*. 5.', L3r), but not 3. The following year, the First Folio contains twenty-nine plays with act or act and scene divisions, whereas seven plays (*2* and *3 Henry VI*, *Troilus and Cressida*, *Titus Andronicus*, *Romeo and Juliet*, *Timon of Athens*, and *Antony and Cleopatra*) are undivided. This evidence suggests that act and scene divisions, where they exist, were added years after the original composition: 'It appears very doubtful . . . that any of the divided plays were originally marked with act headings (except perhaps in the case of *The Tempest*), and that Shakespeare made no regular practice of act division'.[84] On the other hand, some plays clearly do conform to a five-act structure, the most obvious example being *Henry V* where a chorus appears between acts. T. S. Baldwin argued that Shakespeare learnt at school how to construct a play according to the Terentian five-act structure, and the diary of the theatre entrepreneur Philip Henslowe provides clear evidence of the practice of writing plays by acts as early as the 1590s.[85] As for scene divisions, even though they are not marked in any of the early printed editions, they obviously constituted the basic dramatic unit on the early modern stage.

Nicholas Rowe was the first editor who marked act and scene breaks systematically (1709), and modern practice usually derives from the eighteenth century. While many act and scene divisions are unproblematic, others pose problems because some scholars do not agree with the criteria based on which the breaks were introduced and argue that the conventional division obscures the play's shape.[86] *Hamlet* offers a notorious example: Act 4, in a division which Rowe took over from the Sixth Quarto of 1676, begins after Hamlet exits with the body of the dead Polonius, and before the King enters with Rosencrantz and Guildenstern. The Queen remains on stage, and the action is clearly continuous, so that none of the usual criteria for scene division applies. The break was objected to as early as Samuel Johnson, W. W. Greg called it 'a disaster', and many other editors have lamented it while still adhering to it 'in the interests of ease of reference'.[87] This illustrates the two competing claims on the editor in matters of act and scene division: on the one hand, it functions as a reference system which helps students and scholars to communicate with clarity and ease; on the other hand, it serves the purpose, or it ideally serves the purpose, of shedding light on the play's shape.

Which of the two considerations is more important is a matter on which editors disagree. Writing as editor of the Bantam Shakespeare, David Bevington holds that 'we are better off accepting conventional act-scene divisions, since so many works of reference are keyed to them by now, than attempting to impose new act-scene divisions throughout'.[88] The editors of the Oxford *Complete Works*, by contrast, changed quite a number of divisions, though they too stick to the traditional act division in *Hamlet*, 'simply for convenience'.[89] In the Arden 3 *Hamlet*, Ann Thompson and Neil Taylor manage to have it both ways, going along with tradition in the Q2-based main volume but adopting a different solution in the edition of the Folio text in the companion volume.[90]

Questions of scene division may at first seem of minor importance, but anyone who is acquainted with Emrys Jones's study of *Scenic Form in Shakespeare* knows how carefully, and meaningfully, Shakespeare constructed his scenes. In an edition of *The First Quarto of Romeo and Juliet* which I recently completed, this has led me to adopt a new scene division which, I believe, does better justice to the play's shape. The area at issue is what editions traditionally label Act 4, Scene 3; Act 4, Scene 4; and Act 4, Scene 5. In '4.3', Juliet drinks the potion Friar Laurence has given her before falling '*vpon her bed within the Curtaines*' (I1r). '4.4' dramatizes the wedding preparations in the Capulet household, and in '4.5', the

Nurse attempts to wake up Juliet on the morning of her supposed wedding day but, shocked to find her immobile and unconscious, believes her to be dead. The sequence begins and ends with Juliet, and it seems important to recognize that it is continuous, as an editor can suggest by making it one scene. Ronald McKerrow[91] pointed out long ago that the transition from '4.3' to '4.4' is in fact continuous, and Evans similarly noted that the 'scene continues'.[92] Juliet's bed has probably been thrust out from the tiring house and remains onstage at the end of '4.3' when she falls 'upon her bed, within the curtains', meaning the curtains of the canopied bed. Juliet thus remains present on stage, though invisible and immobile, a startling contrast throughout '4.4' to the bustle of the Capulet household: 'make haste, / Make haste' (4.4.26–27). The situation is analogous to the second act of *King Lear*: Kent is put in the stocks ('2.2') and remains onstage during Edgar's soliloquy ('2.3'), following which he is found by Lear ('2.4'), another continuous scene, as a modern edition (e.g. Arden 3) can make clear by disrespecting the traditional scene division.

Concerning the transition from '4.4' to '4.5', Capulet sends the Nurse to wake up Juliet at the end of '4.4' and leaves the stage along with servants, yet the Nurse remains on stage and moves to Juliet's bed, thereby closing the circle opened in '4.3'. Harley Granville-Barker, the great English director and critic of the first half of the twentieth century, strongly objected to an editorial tradition which obscured Shakespeare's grand scenic construction in Act 4 of *Romeo and Juliet*:

> [Juliet's] nurse and her mother leave her; she drinks the potion, and . . . *She falls upon the bed within the curtains* . . . What Shakespeare aims at in the episodes that follow is to keep us conscious of the bed and its burden . . . , till the bridal music is playing, till, to the very sound of this, the Nurse bustles up to draw back the curtains and disclose the girl there stark and still. . . . It is one

scene, one integral stretch of action; and its common mutilation by *Scene IV. Hall in Capulet's House . . . Scene V. Juliet's chambers. Enter Nurse . . .* , is sheer editorial murder.[93]

By not committing this murder, an editor can elucidate the shape of Shakespeare's scenic construction.

Another play whose scene division poses problems is *Macbeth*. The play is among those with act and scene division in the First Folio, and Act 5 is divided into seven scenes: the first six scenes are alternatingly set in Macbeth's castle and the country near Dunsinane, while the last scene begins when Macbeth and Young Siward meet and fight. Among modern editions, Oxford adheres to the Folio but most others do not: the New Penguin edition is content with six scenes in the last act, the Folger instead has eight, to which the New Cambridge adds another one to make it nine, which is still inferior to the number of scenes in the Oxford *Complete Works*: eleven. In fact, all editions agree on what constitutes the first five scenes, the action prior to the battle. Editions differ substantially, however, when it comes to scene divisions from the moment the battle begins. What the difference reveals is that editors do not seem to agree on what, in theory, constitutes a scene. According to a common view, 'A scene is marked by a momentary clearing of the stage'.[94] If this reasoning is applied rigorously, the number of scenes in Act 5 is indeed eleven. Yet according to a different understanding, a scene is a dramatic unit that only ends when either the location changes or time passes. If editors adhere to this view, they have no reason to cut up the battle into several mini-scenes, consisting of as few as fourteen, ten, or even six lines (Oxford *Complete Works*). George Walton Williams has recently urged editors to adopt a solution which corresponds to none of those mentioned above, namely to divide Act 5 into seven scenes, like the Folio, but with a final scene break that is different from the Folio's.[95] What the editorial scene division Williams advocates would make clear to readers is that the penultimate scene corresponds to the action on the battle field (TLN 2378–478), and that the last scene begins after Macbeth has died and his forces capitulated, at the point where 'The accession of the new king is marked triumphantly . . . by Flourish', when a 'change of pace, of business, of location, and of actors' marks the beginning of a new scene.[96] Williams's solution seems simple yet persuasive, suggesting that modern editors of even one of the most famous plays still have the opportunity to reveal Shakespeare's scenic design to the reader with greater clarity than earlier editions have done.

An additional task of the modern editor is to decide on a name for the characters, a name which appears in the edition at the beginning of each speech in what is called the speech heading or speech prefix. Early modern printers used abbreviated names to designate characters, a practice which survived into the twentieth century. Even second series Arden editions still contain speech headings such as '*Sici.*' in *Cymbeline*, '*Cole.*' or '*Moul.*' in *2 Henry IV*, and '*Var. Serv.*', '*Caph.*', and '*Jew.*' in *Timon of Athens*. Those who, like me, would be unable to complete some of these names will agree that the more recent practice adopted in most editions of expanding the abbreviations is an improvement, an editorial intervention that facilitates an easier reading of the plays.

Problems can arise in cases where one and the same character is designated by various speech headings. In *All's Well that Ends Well*, the 'Countess', as modern editions put it, is in fact variously referred to as 'Mother', 'Countess', 'Old Countess', 'Lady', and 'Old Lady' in the First Folio. The character most modern editions call 'Puck' is sometimes called 'Robin' (Goodfellow). Appellations often fluctuate between name and title: Titania and Queen, Hippolyta and Duchess, Theseus and Duke, Lear (or John, Richard, or Henry) or King. Another fluctuation is that between name and racial label: Aaron is also called 'Moor' and Shylock 'Jew'. In these cases (or in most of these cases), the task of the editor will be to choose from among the multiple speech headings. By doing so, the editor risks effacing (or at least relegating to footnotes) potentially important meaning inherent in the original editions,[97] but the convenience of a single label rather than a confusing multitude is understandably the dominant consideration for Shakespeare's modern editors.

The choice between variant speech headings may sometimes be fairly straightforward, but on other occasions it is clearly not. Hamlet's uncle, for instance, is called either 'Claudius' or 'King' in the Second Quarto (1604/5) and the First Folio (1623), so should a modern editor call him 'King', as do Arden 2 and Arden 3, 'Claudius', as in the New Cambridge edition, or 'King Claudius', as in the Oxford *Complete Works*? 'Claudius' is an unusual name for a Danish emperor, a name Shakespeare may have chosen to make us think of the Roman emperor of the same name who was said by some to have been poisoned by his wife Agrippina.[98] By using the name in speech headings, an editor can attempt to activate intertextual meaning to which someone who reads 'King' does not have access. The editorial decision for or against 'Claudius' is all the more significant as the name only appears in a stage direction (in Q2 and F) and a speech heading (in Q2) but never in the dialogue text.

In other cases, the editorial tradition has created a name for a character which is in fact absent from early modern editions. Such, for instance, is the case for 'Lady Capulet', who is variously labelled 'Mother', 'Wife', 'Lady', 'Old Lady', or 'Capulet's Wife' in speech headings (Q2, 1599). Similarly, the character modern editions call 'Lady Macbeth' is variously called 'Macbeths Wife' (TLN 348, 1.5.0), 'Lady' (TLN 647, 2.2.0; TLN 725, 2.2.67; TLN 836, 2.3.82; TLN 2111, 5.1.18), and 'Macbeths Lady' (TLN 1151, 3.2.0), but at no point is she 'Lady Macbeth', a label that goes back to Nicholas Rowe in the early eighteenth century. Similarly, 'Lady Macduff' never bears that name in the Folio, nor, unlike 'Lady

Macbeth', is she ever referred to as 'Lady'. Instead, she is either called 'Macduffes Wife' (TLN 1711) or simply 'Wife' (e.g., TLN 1712). Clearly the label 'Lady Macduff' was invented in analogy to 'Lady Macbeth'. I am not aware of a modern editor who departs from the conventional label established by Rowe in the early eighteenth century, but it is only a matter of time, I believe, until someone restores Folio's 'Macbeth's Wife' and 'Macduff's Wife'.

There are rare cases where a modern editor changes speech headings in the course of the play because of a character's change in title. This can happen when someone ascends the throne (Bolingbroke in *Richard II*) or, on the contrary, is deposed (the protagonist in the same play) or loses her royal title because of divorce (Katherine in *Henry VIII*). The case of *Richard II* is particularly complex and modern editorial practice consequently varies. In the Oxford *Complete Works*, the protagonist is 'King Richard' in the first three acts but 'Richard' in the last two, whereas his opponent is 'Bolingbroke' in Acts 1 to 4 but 'King Henry' in Act 5, which means that throughout the deposition scene (4.1), neither of the two is labelled 'King'. In the Riverside and Arden 3 editions, 'Bolingbroke' similarly becomes 'King Henry' in the last act, but the protagonist remains 'King Richard' throughout the play. Whereas the Oxford *Complete Works* thus have no king in Act 4, Riverside and Arden 3 have two kings in Act 5. In the Craig/Bevington edition, the solution is different again, the protagonist remaining '*K. Rich.*' and his opponent '*Boling.*' throughout the play. (The more recent editions by Bevington alone have 'KING HENRY' in Act 5.) The play raises of course the question of the legitimacy of the deposition, and editors arguably comment upon it by refusing or awarding the title of king to Henry and/or Bolingbroke at various stages of the play.

The obvious critical implications of the choice of speech heading may constitute a useful endpoint to this chapter, in which I have argued that the preparation of the text is the central task for

Shakespeare's modern editors, a task which requires considerable discrimination and can have important critical repercussions. Editors modernize and punctuate, name characters, determine who is present on stage, print speeches in prose or verse, choose specific words at the expense of others, even decide when a character is or is no longer king – and in the process determine what constitutes Shakespeare's works.

2 Framing the Text

An edition in a single-play series such as Arden, New Cambridge, or Oxford requires far more than a text. Indeed, the paratext, meaning the editorial apparatus, usually takes up more space than the text. This point was made strikingly clear in a presentation by a fellow graduate student of mine at Oxford back in the mid-1990s. Having prepared an Arden 2 edition with carefully concealed incisions, he illustrated how much paratext it contains by tearing off all its different parts one after another: off went the annotation, off went the collation, off went the introduction, off went the appendices. All that remained of a substantial book (the edition) was a small, thin booklet (the text).

In the preceding chapter, my survey of editorial interventions in the establishment of the text ended with speech headings and the choices in editorial naming they involve. However, not only speech headings lead an editor to decide on names for characters but also the dramatis personae list, with which the play text is regularly prefixed in modern editions. As with act and scene divisions, the dramatis personae list is largely a product of the editorial tradition. No Shakespeare playbooks published in his lifetime contained such a list, and only seven plays in the First Folio do so (*The Tempest*, *The Two Gentlemen of Verona*, *Measure for Measure*, *The Winter's Tale*, *2 Henry IV*, *Timon of Athens*, and *Othello*), though they are called 'The Actors [sic] Names', 'The Names of the Actors' or 'The Names of all the Actors' (not 'Characters') and are in fact printed after the play text rather than before it. The practice of prefacing the text with the dramatis personae was not unknown, however, and Ben Jonson's Folio *Works* of 1616 prints a list before each play.

How then are modern editors to proceed? They seem to agree that the convenience of a dramatis personae list is such that it is worth printing – and worth printing before, not after, the play text – despite the absence of precedent in Shakespeare's earliest playbooks. The convention is so engrained that we tend to take it for granted, but it is worthwhile reminding ourselves that it constitutes an editorial intervention with important implications. For what the list suggests is that characters exist prior to and independently of the play text.[99] 'How many children had Lady Macbeth?' is the kind of unanswerable question raised by character criticism in the nineteenth and early twentieth centuries, as practised most influentially by A. C. Bradley in *Shakespearean Tragedy* (1904). Many Shakespeareans since L. C. Knights[100] have expressed dissatisfaction with an approach that treats characters as if they were human beings, with an existence beyond the dramatic text. Yet the dramatis personae lists in modern editions arguably encourage this understanding of character which many today reject.

An additional editorial intervention is constituted by the order in which the dramatis personae list arranges the characters. In the First Folio, female characters come last in most lists, segregated from male characters. So *The Two Gentlemen of Verona* begins with the Duke, descends the social ladder all the way to '*Panthion: seruant to Antonio*', and only thereafter mentions Julia, Silvia, and Lucetta, even though Silvia is of course the daughter of the Duke at the top of the list. Modern editions long replicated this gender division, though several critics have lamented the conservatism, or even the misogyny, of traditional practice.[101] While some recent editions still preserve the gender segregation (e.g. Riverside and New Cambridge *Romeo and Juliet*), current practice shows considerable variety. Some editions list characters in the order of appearance (e.g. the New Cambridge *Henry V*). Others list groups of characters: the Capulets and the Montagues in *Romeo and Juliet*, the Athenians, the fairies, and the mechanicals in *A Midsummer Night's Dream*, and so on. Within such groups, some editors list characters according to dramatic importance (Juliet ahead of her parents, e.g. Oxford *Romeo and Juliet*), others according to social hierarchy (Juliet's parents ahead of their daughter, e.g. Arden 2 *Romeo and Juliet*). Other solutions seem equally possible and may be adopted by future editors: an appendix to David and Ben Crystal's *Shakespeare's Words* prints diagrams which 'display the circles within which people move during a play, so that their relationships to each other, either individually or in groups, can be better understood'.[102] No matter how editors present the dramatis personae, they foreground certain information (rank, dramatic importance, structure in terms of character groups, or the relative order in which characters enter) at the expense of other.

Perhaps even more importantly, editors can shape a reader's response to characters by providing or withholding information about them in the dramatis personae list. Should Macbeth be called one of the 'Generals of the King's Army' (Arden 2) or 'thane of Glamis' (Folger) or 'Thane of Glamis, later Thane of Cawdor, later King of Scotland' (New Cambridge)? The first two describe the character at the beginning of the play, one in military, the other in feudal terms, whereas the third charts his progress in the course of the play. Is Othello simply 'the Moor' (Bevington), 'the Moor of Venice' (Oxford *Complete Works*) or 'the Moor, a general in the service of Venice' (New Cambridge)? Or take the example of *As You Like It*: should Rosalind be described as 'daughter of Duke Senior' (Arden 3) or 'daughter to the banished duke' (Craig/Bevington, 1973), or should an editor also announce to the reader that she is 'later disguised as Ganymede' (Bevington, Oxford *Complete Works*)? Is Audrey 'a country girl' (Arden 3), 'a goat-herd' (Arden 2), or 'a country wench' (Bevington)? Is Phoebe best described as a 'shepherdess', or is it better to warn the reader by qualifying that she is 'a disdainful shepherdess' (Folger)? Finally, how about Hymen, the character who appears at the end of the play – we know not how, we know not whence – in a masque-like moment, restoring Rosalind to her father. Is Hymen indeed the 'god of marriage' (Oxford *Complete Works*) or, more prosaically, 'A person representing Hymen' (Riverside)? At least two articles have been written on the subject, one arguing that Hymen *is* a god[103] and another one holding instead that Hymen is Corin in disguise.[104] The question seems difficult to resolve either way, and Agnes Latham perceptively notes that 'It is left to the producer to decide whether the masque shall be plainly a charade got up by Rosalind, or whether it is pure magic, like the masque in *The Tempest*'.[105] How problematic the question is seems to have been recognized by Juliet Dusinberre in the Arden 3 edition who provides explanations for all other characters in her 'list of roles' but leaves a conspicuous blank next to 'Hymen'. As these examples show, editorial dramatis personae lists can have a considerable impact on how readers think of characters.

The most time-consuming part in the making of an editorial apparatus is likely to be the annotation.[106] Although Samuel Johnson considered footnotes 'necessary evils' and warned that the mind would be 'refrigerated by interruption',[107] annotation is key in bridging the historical and cultural divide that separates a late-sixteenth or early-seventeenth-century play from modern readers, all the more so as this divide is growing deeper with the passage of time. Whereas editors still took for granted certain knowledge of the Bible and the classics a few generations ago, they can no longer do so today. As John Pitcher has put it, 'Part of an editor's duty . . . is to ensure that readers and audiences don't forget what *was* obvious to earlier generations about a Renaissance poem or play or novel – even if this means providing a fuller and more elaborate elucidation of the text than we are accustomed to', which means that 'Renaissance writing now requires new levels of editorial annotation to make it intelligible'.[108]

What necessitates more extensive annotation today is not simply that the implied readership is in some ways less knowledgeable but also that it is more diverse. In the eighteenth century, the Shakespeare editor typically aimed his footnotes at fellow editors, whose errors he corrected and whom he often showered with abuse. Judging by the annotation, Shakespeare editing, in other words, was still a semi-private affair among a number of eccentric scholars. In the early twenty-first century, by contrast, 'the anticipated readership of an Arden edition includes senior school pupils, students, teachers, scholars, directors and actors, many of whom will not have English as their first language'.[109] While today's implied readership of editorial annotation is thus more diverse than it used to be, it is also less tolerant towards obfuscation, a significant development considering Shakespeare's language is steeped in bawdy. Many past editors managed to be 'both coy and unhelpful'[110] in annotating – or failing to annotate – Shakespeare's sexual allusions. From modern editors, however, readers rightly expect annotation that is 'impudent . . . in its etymological sense',[111] meaning free from shame. When Hamlet asks Ophelia, 'Do you think I meant country matters?' (3.2.114), the Arden 1 editor 'suspect[ed] . . . some indelicate suggestion in *country*'. The note in Arden 3, by contrast, points out that the line contains 'a pun on "cunt"'. When Hamlet says 'Nothing' a few lines later, Arden 1 suspects no indelicacy, but Arden 3 notes that '"Thing" could be a euphemism for a man's penis'. In producing their annotation, Shakespeare's modern editors thus have the challenging task of mediating local meaning in ways that do justice to Shakespeare's text and to the expectations of an increasingly diverse readership.

All editors strive for annotation that is as useful and clear as possible, yet in their individual practice they can substantially differ from each other and shape readerly response in ways that are distinct. For instance, Laurie Maguire has shown that editors provide glosses that are more or less 'ideologically responsible'.[112]

As Michael Cordner has argued, only some editors are attuned to the performance potential offered by the play.[113] More generally, annotation can privilege the verbal at the expense of the visual, as most traditional editions do, or emphasize the interplay of the visual and the verbal, as some more recent editions do.[114] Consciously or not, editors determine the relative prominence of various kinds of notes, 'textual, etymological, intertextual, contextual, dramatic, or critical'.[115] Of these, the dramatic and critical notes, in particular, can be predominantly descriptive or prescriptive. Cordner and G. K. Hunter have argued against the latter, Cordner arguing that it threatens 'to impose a kind of interpretative certainty upon the text which a playscript by its very nature cannot yield',[116] Hunter holding that 'sophisticated' annotation 'is concerned with questions more than answers, and operates as the interrogator of texts rather than the explainer'.[117]

A feature of a modern edition on which much scholarly energy is spent but which most readers, I suspect, consistently ignore is the collation, a word which does not refer to a light meal or repast but to the record of textual comparison between different editions (OED n.3). In most scholarly series, this record takes the form of a short-hand notation, in small print below the main text, which may at first seem impenetrable. This has given the collation a bad reputation, and it has been variously referred to as the 'band of terror' or the 'barbed wire' between text and footnotes.[118] Yet in fact, the collation is much better than its reputation. For a start, it is in fact quite easy to understand. Here, for instance, is a collation note in the New Cambridge edition of *Henry V*:

14 a babbled of green fields] *Theobald*; a Table of greene fields F; And talk of floures Q

As we have seen, Falstaff is said to have 'babbled of green fields' shortly before his death, according to Mistress Quickly, except that 'a babbled of green fields' is in fact an emendation first proposed by Lewis Theobald in the eighteenth century, taken over in most editions since, including the New Cambridge. So the collation note, after recording the line to which it refers ('**14**'), notes the reading adopted in the modern edition, 'a babbled of green fields', the so-called 'lemma', followed, after the square bracket, by the name of the editor who first adopted the reading (*'Theobald'*). Then, separated by semi-colons, follow the readings which do not make it into the main text. If editions depart from the copy text (as the New Cambridge here does), they first record the reading in the text on which the edition is otherwise based, which, in the case of *Henry V*, is the First Folio (short 'F'): 'a Table of greene fields'. This can be followed by readings from other editions which the editor deems of sufficient interest to be worth recording: 'And talk of floures', the reading in the First, unauthorized (formerly labelled 'bad') Quarto.

It is generally considered the editor's duty to record *all* departures from the quarto or folio copy text. This allows readers to identify where the editor has interfered by means of emendation. A historical collation additionally records other readings adopted (or conjecturally argued for) at some point in the play's editorial history. An exhaustive historical collation seems impossible at this late point in time: there have been hundreds of editions of Shakespeare's plays in the course of the last four centuries, many, though by no means all, of which are listed in Andrew Murphy's impressive *Shakespeare in Print*. The ongoing New Variorum Edition of Shakespeare, published by the Modern Language Association of America, under the general editorship of Richard Knowles and Paul Werstine, provides the fullest historical collation. The most recent volume in the series, *The Winter's Tale* (2005), records all 'significant departures from the F1 text in eighty-six editions of the play ranging in date from 1632 to 1988'.[119] Even the New Variorum Shakespeare, however, needs to be selective in its collation, and a volume in the Arden, Oxford, or New Cambridge series has to be much more so.

The art of the collation note which many of Shakespeare's best editors have mastered thus consists in the selection of the truly interesting variants which serve to enrich the readerly experience. Too many collation notes may drown what is of particular interest amidst what is not. Yet too few collation notes, as Eric Rasmussen has shown, means that the editor passes up the chance of drawing the reader's attention to 'fascinating material' that is 'to be gleaned from what might seem to be an unpromising record of textual variants'.[120] For instance, when Claudius tries to stop the fight between Hamlet and Laertes ('Part them! They are incensed'), Hamlet responds, 'Nay, come, again' (5.2.305–6), which most modern editors punctuate with commas, following Q2's 'come again' and F1's 'come, againe'. Yet the Arden 2 collation note usefully mentions the punctuation in G. L. Kittredge's 1939 edition, 'come! again!', which, albeit heavy-handed, seems an interesting attempt at signalling the excitement of the fight. The following passage similarly gains from a textual note:

MACBETH . . . Come, seeling night,
Scarf up the tender eye of pitiful day,
And with thy bloody and invisible hand
Cancel and tear to pieces that great bond
Which keeps me pale!

(3.2.49–53)

Arden 2 and the Oxford *Complete Works* inform the reader in the collation that Howard Staunton, a nineteenth-century scholar, conjectured that the last word should be 'paled' (meaning 'encircled' or 'surrounded'). There is no evidence for this in any early edition, but the idea of restraint, rather than dread, makes good sense in the given context. If Staunton were right, the Folio reading would be the simple result of an 'e/d' misprint, 'pale' for 'pald', which happened easily enough in the handwriting of the period, called 'secretary hand', in which 'e' and 'd' could look almost alike. These are not grounds for modern editors to emend 'pale' to 'paled', but the reading seems of sufficient interest to merit mention in the collation.

The same applies to Romeo's ecstatic words at the sight of Juliet: 'It seems she hangs upon the cheek of night . . .' (1.5.46). The Second Folio of 1632 substitutes for the first three words, 'Her Beauty', as the New Cambridge collation notes. There is of course no reason to believe that the reading is authorial, but the collation is nonetheless of considerable interest. In particular, it alerts us to the fact that long before the eighteenth century, editors were consciously interfering with Shakespeare's text in the hope of improving it, a point Sonia Massai's recent *Shakespeare and the Rise of the Editor* should do much to establish.[121]

An issue that is directly related to the collation and the commentary is that of the presentation of the textual material. The usual arrangement in scholarly editions of the second half of the twentieth century (as reflected by Arden 2, New Cambridge, and Oxford) is to have the main text at the top of the page, the commentary in smaller type at the bottom, and the collation, in smaller type still, in-between: 'the barbed wire'. In the Arden 3 series, however, the respective place of commentary and collation has been inverted, with the collation having been degraded to the bottom of the page, perhaps a reflection of its perceived unimportance. Another arrangement is that of the Folger and the recently reissued Bantam Shakespeare, where text and annotation appear on facing pages. A more fundamental decision concerning the textual presentation is whether commentary and/or collation should appear on the same double page at all, the alternative being that they appear at the back of the book (as in the New Penguin series) or in a separate volume (as in the *Textual Companion* of the

Oxford *Complete Works*). Even though Noël Coward thought that 'having to read footnotes was like having to go downstairs to answer the door when upstairs making love',[122] many readers no doubt find it convenient to be able to glance to the foot of the page rather than having to turn the pages in search for information. Yet a clean-page format also offers advantages: more text fits on a page, and the editor runs no risk of drowning the text in annotation. The latter consideration is what accounts for the arrangement in editions – like the Arden 2 *Hamlet* – which provide commentary at the bottom of the page *and* in the back of the book. Shorter notes appear below the text, longer notes at the end of it.

Whereas annotation and collation often figure on the same page as the text, there is a lot more paratext elsewhere in editions like the Arden. First and foremost, the introduction. Perhaps no other part of an edition can do more to shape a reader's response to the play. To a certain extent, this is inevitable: space being limited, introductions are necessarily 'partial', as it were, privileging certain aspects over others. Yet this partiality is also the result of a historical development which has recently led to greater editorial scope in shaping introductions. Roughly half a century ago, the early Arden 2 editions had introductions with a fairly well-defined structure: discussions of 'text', 'date', and 'sources' usually came first, typically followed by sections devoted to themes and earlier criticism. Not that the structure of all introductions was identical, but, clearly, there was a standard structure which gave pride of place to what many today would consider fairly dry points of scholarship. By contrast, the first long section in the introduction to the Arden 3 *As You Like It* deals with 'Fictions of gender' (9–36); the introduction to the Arden 3 *King Lear* begins with a massive section on 'Reading and staging *King Lear*' (3–80); and the first fifty pages of the introduction to the Arden 3 *Richard II* deal with 'Politics' (5–55). Issues such as date and sources are typically confined to a less prominent position or lumped together under 'Origins' or 'Inception', as in the Arden 3 *Titus Andronicus* and *King Lear*. Whereas for much of the twentieth century, editors tried to function in introductions as supposedly objective conveyors of scholarly 'facts and problems', they no longer shy away today from being self-consciously subjective interpreters, with their critical preferences and blind spots. This applies not only to Arden: in the New Cambridge series, for instance, the introduction to *Macbeth* contains a thought-provoking section on '*Macbeth* in the mind and in performance: Act 4, Scene 3' (88–93), which reads like a short essay presenting an original argument. As a result of the historical changes in the structure and purpose of introductions, editors today have maximum impact on the plays' reception by mediating to readers not only past scholarly wisdom but also present critical opinion.

The length of introductions goes hand in hand with these changes. The introductions to *Love's Labour's Lost* count thirty-two pages in Arden 2 but 106 in Arden 3. The Arden 2 *Lear* introduction had fewer than fifty, the Arden 3 *Lear* more than 150 pages. *Henry VIII* has seen its introduction grow from fifty-three pages in Arden 2 to almost 200 in Arden 3. Clearly, Arden 2 introductions got longer as the series was appearing, which explains why the introduction to *King Lear*, published in 1952, has less than one third of the length of that to *The Taming of the Shrew* in 1981. A logical correlative of the editors' increased contribution was that editions – like monographs – started having an index in the Oxford and Arden 3 series.

Related to this development in length is the prominence given to the play in performance. Stage histories were not entirely absent from Arden 2, but their importance remained marginal, three to five pages being an acceptable length, as exemplified by the Arden 2 *The Merchant of Venice* of 1955 (xxxii-xxxvi), *Henry VIII* of 1957 (lxii-lxv), *Pericles* of 1963 (lxv-lxix), or *As You Like It* of 1967 (lxxxvi-xci). The Arden 2 *Lear* (1952) spends less than two pages on the play on stage, from Richard Burbage to Laurence Olivier (xliii-xlv), which is still more than the Arden 2 *Macbeth* (1951), which squeezed it into one short paragraph: 'Most of the great actors and actresses during the past three hundred years have appeared in *Macbeth*, from Burbage to Mr. John Gielgud; but between 1674 and 1744 the play was performed only in D'Avenant's adaptation. Garrick restored most of Shakespeare's text and Macready most of the rest' (xliv). The contrast to recent editions could not be starker. The 'stage history' in the New Cambridge *Coriolanus* (2000) exceeds thirty pages, the 'Performance History' in the Oxford *Romeo and Juliet* (2000) has more than forty pages, and that in the Arden 3 *Henry VIII* (2000) amounts to fifty pages. Even *Troilus and Cressida* – not a play known for its staginess – receives a stage history of more than thirty pages in Arden 3 (1998). In keeping with the increased attention devoted to the play in performance, appendices in many Arden 3 volumes provide a casting chart. Typical appendices in the Arden 2 series, by contrast, dealt with the plays' sources. Whereas editors of earlier series thus largely confined themselves to how the plays fared on the page, modern editors also describe in some detail their fortune on stage. Most recently, Shakespeare on screen is now coming into prominence, notably in a separate section in the recently reissued Bantam Shakespeare (2005).

On some occasions, editors also have to decide on the title of the play they edit: *Anthony and Cleopatra* or *Antony and Cleopatra*? Stanley Wells, the general series editor of the Oxford Shakespeare, is on record as having tried to dissuade Michael Neill from the spelling 'Anthony', but Neill persisted.[123] Similarly, should it be *Love's Labour's* [or *Labor's*] *Lost* (as most modern editions have it) or *Love's Labours Lost*? As Henry Woudhuysen points out, 'If the apostrophe in "*Labor's*" is correct, then the title means "the labour of love is lost" rather than "the lost labours of love"'.[124] In other words, the choice of title matters. Interestingly, the early Quarto and Folio editions contain multiple possibilities – 'Loues Labour lost' (First

Folio content page), 'Loues Labour's lost' (First Folio title and running header), 'Loues labors lost' (Q1 title page), and 'Loues Labor's lost' (Q1 running header) – but never adopt the spelling favoured in most modern editions: *Love's Labour's Lost*. Furthermore, is the last part of Shakespeare's second tetralogy called *Henry V* (Oxford) or *King Henry V* (New Cambridge) or *The Life of Henry V* (Oxford *Complete Works*)? The play hardly gives the impression that it tries to cover the entire life, but the recent tendency, as evidenced by the Oxford *Complete Works* and Bate and Rasmussen, seems to be towards '*The Life of Henry V*', which is closest to the title in the Folio: 'The Life of Henry the Fift'. Is it *King Henry VI, Part II* or *Two* (Arden 3 and Oxford) or *The Second Part of Henry VI* (New Cambridge) or *The First Part of the Contention of the Two Famous Houses of York and Lancaster* (Oxford *Complete Works*)? Is it *Henry VIII* (Bowers, ed., *The Dramatic Works in the Beaumont and Fletcher Canon*) or *King Henry VIII* (Arden 3 and Oxford) or *King Henry the Eighth* (New Penguin) or *The Life of King Henry the Eighth* (Berdan and Brooke, eds., Yale Shakespeare) or *All Is True* (Oxford *Complete Works*)? And so on.

Some of these differences may seem fairly insignificant, but others are not. *King Henry VIII* has a different generic resonance from *All Is True*. With the title *King Henry VIII*, the Folio places the play in the company of the English histories of the 1590s, whereas *All Is True* (as the play seems originally to have been referred to) may align it with the romances with which the play's late date accords. Or take *The Second Part of Henry VI*. This title suggests the play is a sequel, whereas *The First Part of the Contention of the Two Famous Houses of York and Lancaster* implies, on the contrary, that the play will be followed by a sequel. *The Second Part of Henry VI* places the play in the Folio's trilogy of *Henry VI* plays, whereas *The First Part of the Contention*, in conformity with the play's publication (and probably performance) history during Shakespeare's lifetime, puts it alongside *The True Tragedy of Richard Duke of York* (what the Folio calls *The Third Part of Henry VI*), with which it appeared in print in 1619 as the first part of a diptych called *The Whole Contention between the Two Famous Houses, Lancaster and York*. Yet the Quarto text of *The First Part of the Contention of the Two Famous Houses of York and Lancaster* is rather different from the text in the Folio, and even the editors of the Oxford *Complete Works* base their edition on the latter, despite the fact that they adopt the title of the former. What's in a title?

Beyond all the choices that concern editors of individual plays, series editors, like general editors of complete works, have to take a number of additional decisions of which a couple may be addressed here. A preliminary decision is not only *how* to edit plays but also *what* plays to edit: the thirty-six First-Folio plays and *Pericles*, of course. *The Two Noble Kinsmen*, probably (though Bevington did not include it until the updated 4th edition of 1997, and no edition has been published in the New Cambridge series). But how about *Edward III*? In (New Cambridge; Riverside 2nd ed.; Oxford *Complete Works* 2nd ed.) or out (Riverside 1st ed.; Oxford *Complete Works* 1st ed.; Bevington, Bate and Rasmussen). If *Edward III* becomes a canonical Shakespeare play, as recent developments suggest, should we stop referring to 'Shakespeare's second tetralogy' and instead start talking about 'Shakespeare's pentalogy'? And what of *Sir Thomas More* – include the play as a whole (Arden 3, Oxford *Complete Works* 2nd ed.), provide only the passages attributed to Shakespeare (Riverside, Bate and Rasmussen, Oxford *Complete Works* 1st ed.), or omit it altogether (Bevington, New Cambridge)? Might it even make sense to include, as the Arden 3 series is planning to do, an edition of Lewis Theobald's *Double Falsehood* on the basis that it may be an eighteenth-century adaptation of the lost Shakespeare/Fletcher play *Cardenio* (even though E. K. Chambers was rather sceptical about this theory)?[125] A recent article by an established scholar forcefully argues that Shakespeare wrote one scene, the so-called Quarrel Scene, of the anonymous

Arden of Faversham.[126] Will a future edition of Shakespeare's complete works include *Arden of Faversham*?

Editors of complete works not only need to decide on a corpus but also on how to order it. Few editions in the past centuries have done what the *Arden Shakespeare Complete Works* of 1998 does, namely to start the dramatic corpus with *All's Well That Ends Well* and *Antony and Cleopatra*, and end it with *The Two Noble Kinsmen* and *The Winter's Tale*, simply arranging the plays in alphabetical order. The First Folio divides the plays by genre into comedies, histories, and tragedies. The *Complete Works* by Bate and Rasmussen follows this arrangement, adding everything else at the end, including the poems. Yet the Folio's generic division is clearly not the one favoured by most modern scholars, who usually distinguish between the comedies and the late romances. Even those who do not would hardly place *Cymbeline* among the tragedies, as the Folio does. In addition, there is the problem of *Troilus and Cressida*, which heads the tragedies but has also variously been considered a comedy, a history, or a tragicomedy. It is of course possible to 'correct' the First Folio but to preserve the basic organization by genre, as in Riverside or Bevington: comedies, histories, tragedies, romances, poems. Alternatively, genre can be disposed of altogether as a structuring principle and chronology adopted instead, the solution favoured by the Oxford *Complete Works*.

The question of chronology is of course no less vexed than the question of genre, so organization by chronology leads to other tough decisions, as can be gathered from the fact that the editors of the Oxford *Complete Works* changed their minds in several respects between the first and the second edition. Was *1 Henry VI* written before *Titus Andronicus* (2nd ed.) – and thus directly after *2* and *3 Henry VI* – or after (1st ed.)? Did Shakespeare write *Richard II* after *Romeo and Juliet* and *A Midsummer Night's Dream* (1st ed.) or before (2nd ed.)? The earlier version of the chronology may suggest that Shakespeare, in the mid-1590s, proceeded by clusters of plays:

first *Love's Labour's Lost* and the (lost?) *Love's Labour's Won*; then *A Midsummer Night's Dream* and *Romeo and Juliet*, sister plays with 'extraordinary parallels between them at every level of style and structure';[127] and finally two history plays, *Richard II* and *King John*. Yet if *Richard II* is moved back, the chronology does not support such a hypothesis. And how about *All's Well That Ends Well*? Was it written before *Timon of Athens*, *The History of King Lear*, *Macbeth*, and *Antony and Cleopatra* (1st ed.), or was it written after these four tragedies (2nd ed.)? The earlier chronology suggests a generic progression in the course of the 1600s from comedy to tragedy to romances; the more recent chronology violates such a view by placing *All's Well That Ends Well* after most of the tragedies and right before *Pericles*, the earliest romance.

From the modernization of spelling and punctuation to the inclusion and arrangement of the material in complete works, editors of Shakespeare decisively shape his plays, suggesting one meaning, or one reading, rather than another, collectively enriching the modern readers' understanding and response to Shakespeare's texts. After the survey of the range of editorial collaboration in the first two chapters, the next chapter turns to a single issue, the important matter of the editorial treatment of stage directions.

3 Editing Stage Action

The preceding chapter has examined editorial interventions in all their breadth. This chapter looks at a single issue in greater depth: the modern editorial mediation of stage action. In keeping with the general aim of *Shakespeare's Modern Collaborators*, my goals in this chapter are to demonstrate that, firstly, editorial intervention is of far-reaching importance in mediating Shakespearean stage action to today's readers; secondly, even though editors may vigorously disagree as to how exactly stage action is best conveyed to modern readers, their impact is fundamentally enabling; and, thirdly, some of the issues at stake in the question of how to edit stage action are of such complexity that we have a vested interest in familiarizing ourselves with them if we wish to become more sophisticated users of modern editions.

In Shakespeare's early modern playbooks, stage action is generally signalled by explicit or implied stage directions. An example of an explicit stage direction is Antigonus's exit in *The Winter's Tale*, '*pursued by a bear*' (3.3.57); an example of an implicit stage direction is Gloucester's ''tis most ignobly done / To pluck me by the beard' (*King Lear* 3.7.36–37). Although Gloucester's words are not accompanied by an explicit stage direction, they nevertheless make clear that a stage action has preceded them. Stage directions as well as implied stage directions often prompt modern editorial intervention of some kind. Many stage directions are perceived to be unclear or even erroneous, causing editors to intervene by changing, adding, omitting, transposing, and annotating the stage directions in the early editions. Implied stage directions, even when they make clear that stage action of some kind occurs, often leave it unclear what exactly this action is, when and how often it happens, by whom it is carried out, and so on.

What adds to the complexity of the modern editorial mediation of stage action is the relative scarcity of stage directions in early modern playbooks. Used to the frequent and detailed stage directions of modern dramatists, modern readers can be surprised by the paucity of such directions in the early playbooks of Shakespeare and his contemporaries. We know about the Elizabethans' predilection for stage action, for clowning, and for pageantry, and there is no doubt that these plays, when performed, contained far more action than is recorded in stage directions. Anthony Hammond has argued that 'ninety percent of what actually happened on stage in their performance is not to be found in the stage-directions of any manuscript or printed text',[128] a point with which the stage historian Alan Dessen agrees when similarly arguing that as much as ninety per cent of the 'relevant evidence' for stage action of the early performances of Shakespeare's plays is irretrievably lost.[129]

What these estimates by two experts can tell us is that early modern readers may have had rather different expectations about a playbook from those of modern readers. Recent editorial practice suggests that many modern readers expect (and modern editors strive to provide) a surrogate performance, a text which allows readers to imagine a performance in the mind. What we know about early modern reading practices and what we can infer from early modern playbooks is that sixteenth- and seventeenth-century readers of dramatic texts particularly appreciated poetic passages, 'purple patches', which they highlighted or excerpted, passages which make for good, literary reading. By contrast, inferring the theatrical content from the text does not seem to have been a priority of early modern readers. In the words of M. J. Kidnie, 'Shakespeare's stage directions seem to have conformed, as far as we can tell, to early modern theatrical standards of textual completeness and correctness. These scripts, in other words, are not deficient in any absolute or transhistorical sense. They just seem deficient to us'.[130]

In view of this deficiency, it has long been generally accepted 'that the editor of a critical edition has a responsibility to amplify the directions of his original texts',[131] thereby helping modern readers to visualize, imaginatively, the play in performance. *The Winter's Tale* offers an instructive example: convinced that the baby to whom Hermione has given birth is the fruit of an adulterous relationship with Polixenes, Leontes banishes the new-born from his court, ordering Antigonus to abandon it far from Sicily. When Antigonus reluctantly does so, he speaks the following lines (I quote from the First Folio, the play's only substantive early edition):

> There lye, and there thy character: there these,
> Which may if Fortune please, both breed thee (pretty)
> And still rest thine.
>
> (TLN 1489–91)

What 'these' and 'thy character' refer to is obvious for a spectator but at first impossible to know for a reader with no editorial assistance. It is not until later in this scene, after Antigonus has left the stage 'pursued by a bear' and after a shepherd has found the baby, that we learn that 'these' designate gold and jewels left in a box. In Act 5, Scene 2, finally, we find out that 'thy character' refers to letters written by Antigonus. These objects are not incidental to the plot. In the penultimate scene, two gentlemen at Leontes' court discuss the plausibility of the newly broken news of the babe's restoration. 'This news', the Second Gentleman says, 'is so like an old tale that the verity of it is in strong suspicion' (5.2.28–30). Not so, the Third Gentleman replies, for the gold, the jewels, and the letters found with the babe allow for unambiguous identification

(5.2.33–36). Shakespeare thus needs the props in Act 3, Scene 3 to authenticate Perdita's recovery in the last act. As a consequence, Bevington prints the passage as follows:

> [*He lays down the baby.*]
> There lie, and there thy character; there these,
>   [*He places a box and a fardel beside the baby.*]
> Which may, if fortune please, both breed thee, pretty,
> And still rest thine.
>
> (3.3.45–47)

In the Oxford *Complete Works* similar stage directions are added:

> *He lays down the babe and a scroll*
> There lie, and there thy character.
>   *He lays down a box*
>   There these,
> Which may, if fortune please, both breed thee, pretty,
> And still rest thine.
>
> (3.3.46–48)

By inserting stage directions into the text, the editors provide information 'at a point equivalent to that at which its visual correlative would be apprehended in the theatre'.[132] The information is essential for an understanding of the passage at the time it is read, and editions, like the one in the Arden 2 series, that fail to include a direction, arguably abnegate editorial responsibility by providing a text which they could have rendered intelligible but did not.

The central question in the following instance seems at first straightforward: Who is on stage? For whom, in other words, do the stage directions have to provide an entrance?[133] At the beginning of the second scene of *The Winter's Tale*, the stage direction in the First Folio reads as follows: '*Enter Leontes, Hermione, Mamil-*

lius, *Polixenes, Camillo*' (TLN 49). Lewis Theobald believed that these characters enter '*with attendants*', and most modern editors, following Theobald, add the words 'and attendants' between square brackets. The motivation behind this addition is understandable: with two kings and a queen on stage, we would normally expect to have attendants present. Moreover, it is not unusual for less important characters like attendants not to be mentioned in stage directions in early editions, even when the context makes clear they are on stage. On the other hand, it seems important to notice that nothing in the dialogue suggests that this is a state occasion. The whole of Act 1, Scene 2 can be understood as a private scene, and some modern productions have interpreted it as such.[134]

The difference in staging matters profoundly. At the heart of this scene Hermione persuades Polixenes, King of Bohemia, to stay longer in Sicily as their guest, thereby triggering her husband Leontes' jealousy. As long as we read editions (or see productions) in which it is conceived as a *public* scene, it is easy to assume that the sudden emergence of Leontes' jealousy is partly caused by the fact that the Queen is displaying her intimacy with Polixenes in public. Accordingly, his excessive reaction may be seen in relation to his mistaken belief not only in his wife's infidelity but also in his public exposition as a cuckold. However, such a view would be conditioned by the stage directions in modern editions and productions based on them, by modern editorial intervention rather than on what the extant textual witnesses bear out. We need to beware, of course, of imposing a modern notion of privacy upon this scene if we are striving for an adequate historical understanding. Yet in any case, how exactly we imagine the workings of Leontes' diseased imagination, leading to all the complications that make up *The Winter's Tale*, can clearly be related to whether editorial stage directions construe this scene as essentially private or public.

Another scene in which modern editorial intervention decisively shapes the readerly reception by deciding who is on stage is the Capulets' feast in *Romeo and Juliet*. At the beginning of this episode, with Romeo, Mercutio, and Belvolio already on stage, the frustratingly imprecise stage direction reads: '*Enter all the guests and gentlewomen to the Maskers*' (Q2, C3r). It is not easy to determine who is thus entering at this point.[135] Capulet, the next character who speaks, is clearly present, even though he is the host rather than a guest. Other speeches are assigned to Capulet's Cousin, Tybalt, and Juliet, who are thus also on stage. Yet how about the Nurse? As a member of the Capulet household, she is hardly a guest, nor is she a gentlewoman. She speaks later in the scene, though not for another hundred lines. So does she enter at this point or later in the scene? Furthermore, when the Nurse does finally speak, she addresses Juliet to ask her to see her mother: 'Madam, your mother craves a word with you' (1.5.112). Does that mean that Juliet's mother is not on stage? It seems reasonable to assume that she is, but it is worthwhile pointing out that nothing in the text allows us to settle the question. Finally, what about Count Paris? In Act 1, Scene 2, he was invited to the feast by Capulet:

> This night I hold an old accustomed feast,
> Whereto I have invited many a guest
> Such as I love; and you among the store,
> One more, most welcome, makes my number more.
> (1.2.20–23)

Paris has an excellent reason to be present at the feast, but he never speaks throughout the scene, nor does an exit or entrance indicate his presence. Much is made of Romeo's rival at the Capulets' feast in a number of modern productions as well as in the film versions of Franco Zeffirelli and Baz Luhrmann. Yet what we know about the size of Shakespeare's company and about the amount of doubling practised at the time makes it seem possible that the actor playing Paris originally played a different part during this scene and that the Count was thus not among the guests.[136]

The problem is so complex that it is difficult to find two modern editions adopting the same solution. Some preserve the vagueness of the original: '*Enter Capulet, attendants, and all the guests and gentlewomen to the masquers*' (Oxford). This adds 'Capulet' and 'attendants' to the stage direction in Q2 but does not specify several other characters, including Juliet, whom we are presumably meant to count among the 'gentlewomen'. Similarly, Bevington has '*Enter* [Capulet *and family and*] *all the guests and gentlewomen to the masquers*', which singles out not only Capulet but the Capulet 'family', yet fails to provide an entrance for Tybalt's Page, who speaks later in the scene. The New Cambridge edition seems to show awareness of this, as suggested by the more detailed stage direction, '*Enter* [CAPULET, LADY CAPULET, JULIET, TYBALT *and his* PAGE, NURSE, *and*] *all the* GUESTS *and* GENTLEWOMEN *to the Maskers*'. This spells out which characters 'Capulet and family' refer to and provides an entrance for Tybalt's Page, though the question of Paris's presence is left open. The Arden 2 edition is similarly specific when it comes to the Capulet family but, like Bevington, provides no explicit entrance for Tybalt's Page: '*Enter* [CAPULET, LADY CAPULET, JULIET, TYBALT, NURSE *and*] *all the* Guests *and* Gentlewomen *to the Masquers*'. The most elaborate attempt at specifying who enters at this stage is undertaken in the Oxford *Complete Works*: '*Enter* [*Musicians, then*] ... *Capulet,* [*his Wife,*] *his Cousin, Juliet,* [*the Nurse,*] *Tybalt, his page, Petruccio, and all the guests and gentlewomen*'. According to a Q2 stage direction some lines further on, '*Musick playes* (C3r)', and musicians are also present at the end of Act 4, where three of them have speaking parts, valid reasons, it seems, for the Oxford editors to provide an entrance for musicians at this point. The other remarkable addition to the stage direction is 'Petruccio' (spelled 'Petruchio' in most modern editions). The character does not speak but is referred to by name late in the scene:

JULIET   Come hither, Nurse. What is yond gentleman?
NURSE   The son and heir of old Tiberio.
JULIET   What's he that now is going out of door?
NURSE   Marry, that, I think, be young Petruchio.
(1.5.129–32)

Petruchio reappears in a stage direction in Act 3, Scene 1, '*Enter Tybalt, Petruchio, and others*' (3.1.33), but here too the part is a mute one. Does that mean that a stage direction needs to signal Petruchio's presence at the Capulet feast, as the editors of the Oxford *Complete Works* believe? If so, how about the 'son and heir of old Tiberio' who leaves the feast at the same time as Petruchio? If an entrance is provided for Petruchio, why not for Tiberio's son, too? Just how exactly an editor ought to edit the Capulets' feast and the question of who is present at it raises an almost infinite number of questions. What this means is that modern editors can have a considerable interpretative impact by deciding who is, who is not, and who may be present at the Capulets' feast.

In another passage in the same play, the editor's intervention can have important repercussions on our understanding of gender roles in *Romeo and Juliet*. In Act 3, Scene 3, Friar Laurence informs Romeo of his banishment from Verona. Romeo laments his bad fortune and throws himself to the ground before the Nurse enters with news about Juliet. As Romeo attempts to stab himself, the Friar shouts 'Hold thy desperate hand' (3.3.108) before reproaching him for his effeminate behaviour: 'Thy tears are womanish . . . / Unseemly woman in a seeming man' (3.3.110–12). In Q2, on which modern editions are usually based, no stage direction explains what action accompanies the Friar's shout. Most modern productions and films have the Friar intervene by holding back Romeo's arm. Yet in the unauthorized First Quarto of 1597, a stage direction explains that when Romeo '*offers to stab himselfe*', the '*Nurse snatches the dagger away*' (Q1, G1v). The Nurse's intervention is highly resonant: she acts at the crucial moment, though she says little (she interjects 'Ah!' in Q1) or nothing (as in Q2). Friar Laurence, by contrast, sermonizes Romeo in a lengthy passage, but, Q1 suggests, he does not act when it most matters. In addition, the Friar's comments on Romeo's effeminate behaviour follow right after the Nurse's intervention. The Friar claims that 'tears are womanish' at the same time as Q1 shows a woman who acts at a key moment, a man who merely talks, and another man who weeps.

Given that modern editions are generally based on Q2, not on Q1, what are modern editors to do? They generally adopt one of two positions: the one is exemplified by the New Cambridge edition, which simply integrates the stage direction from the First Quarto. The Arden 2 edition, by contrast, provides no stage direction and explains in a footnote that 'There is nothing in the dialogue (or the characterization of the Nurse generally) to prepare for or to support this intervention by the Nurse'. This second option may seem problematic: *Romeo and Juliet* incisively dramatizes gender distinctions and has the male protagonist end with the traditionally feminine suicide (poison) and Juliet with the traditionally masculine suicide (she stabs herself with a dagger). Silencing in such a way a fascinating reading from one of the early editions which further complicates the play's interrogation of masculinity and femininity constitutes a considerable loss. On the other hand, if we believe that Q1 and Q2 both have their own logic and integrity, an editor who integrates the Q1 stage direction into a Q2-based edition runs the risk of conflating two versions which should be kept separate.

As the previous example illustrates, the treatment of stage directions in modern editions can be particularly complicated in cases where several versions of a play are extant and differ significantly. Such is also the case with *Hamlet* of which there are three early versions, the First Quarto of 1603, the Second Quarto of 1604, and the First Folio of 1623. The earliest text is probably an abridged stage adaptation which used to be referred to as a 'bad quarto'. Modern versions are usually based on either the Second Quarto or the First Folio editions, so these are the texts I focus upon. Here is the passage dramatizing Hamlet's death as it appears in G. R. Hibbard's Oxford edition (1987):

HAMLET   O, I die, Horatio.
        The potent poison quite o'ercrows my sprit.
        I cannot live to hear the news from England,
        But I do prophesy th'election lights
        On Fortinbras. He has my dying voice.
        So tell him, with the occurrents, more and less,
        Which have solicited – the rest is silence.
                He gives a long sigh and dies

HORATIO
        Now cracks a noble heart. Good night, sweet prince,
        And flights of angels sing thee to thy rest.

                                                                  (5.2.305–13)

What is bound to capture the attention of readers is the stage direction inserted after Hamlet's famous last words: '*He gives a long sigh and dies*'. Hibbard's stage direction is disconcerting insofar as a long tradition of *Hamlet*s on stage and on the page has accustomed us to taking Hamlet's last words literally and to expecting after them what Hamlet announces, namely silence. So why does he sigh in this edition? And why is it a *long* sigh?

In search of an answer, we turn to the early editions of the play. The Second Quarto is generally considered to be the version that is closest to what Shakespeare originally composed. In this version there is no indication of Hibbard's long sigh. Hamlet's dying words immediately precede Horatio's lines, with no stage direction intervening. In the Folio, however, 'the rest is silence' is followed by four Os separated by commas and the stage direction '*Dyes*'. The four Os seem likely to reflect the sounds produced by Shakespeare's fellow actor, Richard Burbage, who first performed the role of the Danish prince. In fact, what has happened is that Hibbard has interpreted the four Os in the Folio as standing for a long sigh and has translated them into a stage direction. In other words, Hibbard has done nothing less than script the way Shakespeare's most famous character dies.

Hibbard's stage direction is a strongly interpretative editorial intervention, for the onomatopoeic signs, 'O, o, o, o', can surely be construed in a variety of ways: 'a murmur? a wonder? a laugh? a shock? a groan?'[137] As Dieter Mehl has put it, 'the wonderfully rich rhetoric of the Prince has faded into inarticulate sound before it is finally reduced to silence',[138] so the nature of this 'inarticulate sound' seems of some importance as it will inevitably guide our interpretation of Hamlet's end in one way or another. The carefully prepared performance into which John Donne turned his own death can illustrate that 'making a good end' was considered of utmost importance in early modern England, indeed as the key to the evaluation of a person's entire life. A final 'long sigh' allows for a rather different interpretation of Hamlet's life and death than agonized groans would. Both seem different from a silent death, as suggested by the Second Quarto. So the question Hibbard's stage direction raises is that of the boundary between explaining the stage action so that readers can visualize it and interpreting it.

This question is also at the heart of the following example: when Polonius says to Claudius and Gertrude, 'Take this from this, if this be otherwise' (2.2.156), a reader who has never seen the play in performance may at first fail to understand what Polonius means. The first 'this' may be spoken with Polonius pointing to his head and the second with him pointing to his shoulder, Polonius thus saying that the King may behead him if he is not telling the truth (or, as Poins puts it in *1 Henry IV*, 'if you and I do not rob them, cut this head off from my shoulders', 1.2.161–62). Accordingly, what the Riverside and the Arden 2 editions do is insert a stage direction between square brackets reading '*Points to his head and shoulder*'. The Oxford *Complete Works* adds a similar stage direction according to which Polonius is '*touching his head, then his shoulder*'. Thanks to the added stage direction, a reader can visualize stage action that is required for a full understanding of the spoken words. However, Polonius may also be pointing to his staff of office and to his hand, as Edward Dowden suggested, or to his chain of office and his neck, as the Folger edition notes, meaning, in other words, 'deprive me of my *office* if I'm wrong', which, as most people would agree, is rather different from being beheaded.[139] Of course, there is no way of deciding between what seem equally plausible and performable staging options.

The crucial question these passages raise thus is: what is an editor to do when an added stage direction would help readers visualize the stage action yet when the text in the early edition(s) allows for multiple staging options? The answer to this question has important repercussions on the modern editorial mediation of stage action, yet scholars show little agreement in the answers they give. One position is exemplified by George Walton Williams: 'every editor should be a director, whose page is his stage . . . directing the acted word by means of stage directions printed in the text is a task that an editor should regularly perform'.[140] Williams acknowledges that many passages allow for different stagings, but he affirms that a 'directorial function of the editor is to describe what the actors may do on stage . . . when the dialogue is ambiguous and the editor wishes the situation to be unambiguous, a direction is justified'.[141] This affirmation may seem to beg the question insofar as an editor might precisely not want a situation to be unambiguous, but Williams goes on to argue even more forcefully that an editor *should* disambiguate stage action: 'each director has one choice only. Editors must make that same choice, but they may explain in the commentary why they have made that choice and what the other choices are'.[141] This position is endorsed by R. A. Foakes who argues for even greater scope in directorial editing: 'George Walton Williams would encourage editors to emend and provide a correct direction where directions are absent or misleading in early printed texts. I would go further and suggest that editors should be encouraged to take more liberties in suggesting possible action.'[143] Quite clearly, Williams and Foakes hold that it is for an editor to decide how Hamlet dies, or what Polonius points to, by inserting the desired stage direction into the text.

Other scholars have disagreed, and this for various reasons. There are those who wonder just how well suited editors are to function as directors. A. R. Braunmuller warns that 'persons equipped to make good editions of old plays are . . . rarely equipped (or at best only intermittently equipped) to understand matters of performance to the same standard'.[144] Similarly, David Scott Kastan writes that 'I don't believe it is the role of an edition to block the play. Directors and actors have theatrical imaginations far better suited to this task than most editors'.[145] The concept of theatrical imagination is thought-provoking. If directors and actors (and, indeed, readers in general) want to be able to exercise this imagination, they may first need editions that appeal to it. In other words, if an editor makes a directorial choice and embeds it into the text, it may be wondered whether many readers will deactivate their imagination and accept as an incontrovertible feature of the play what may in fact be an arbitrary decision by an editor. M. J. Kidnie has forcefully argued that directorial editing 'erases the textual evidence with which readers trained to read dramatic text are enabled to construct an interpretation of staging independent of the editor's'.[146] Whereas Williams conflates directing and editing (an editor should act like a director), Kidnie opposes them, arguing that editors enable imaginative directing (on stage or in the mind) when they refrain from imposing a decision on the text in passages that contain various staging options.

For similar reasons, John Cox advocates editions that refrain from adding stage directions to the text and instead explicate the performance potential in the annotation: 'My suggestion is that editors reduce sharply or even eliminate completely the stage directions they add to early texts. In place of stage directions in the text, this practice outlines staging options in the commentary notes, thus leaving the text free of editorial interventions where stage directions are concerned while giving readers enough information to imagine various solutions to staging.'[147] A potential problem with Cox's solution is that while added stage directions are immediately noticed by a reader and therefore provide the desired assistance, commentary notes can easily be passed over. Modern editions of Shakespeare's plays typically provide more paratext than text, in particular notes of various kinds, textual, intertextual, lexical/philological, and so on, which not all readers pause to scrutinize when they read the play. As a consequence, further notes about the performance potential of certain lines and passages might well end up being less immediately useful for precisely those readers who are most in need of editorial assistance. This is why Braunmuller evokes Cox's proposed solution only to reject it: 'An editor might write a note canvassing the possibilities as that editor understood them and leave the text as is. This choice is utopian because nobody reads notes, and without a visible sign in the text, the line will remain extremely puzzling. And when I say "nobody reads notes," I especially do not mean undergraduate students or novice Shakespeareans. I mean "nobody".'[148] Even if we do not share Braunmuller's pessimism about readers' interest in notes, it remains true that many readers are likely to sweep past certain stage actions unless the main text alerts them to it.

The position exemplified by Williams's recent essay was in fact advocated by Stanley Wells as early as 1984: 'the editor needs to identify points at which additional directions, or changes to those of the early texts, are necessary to make the staging intelligible'.[149] The Oxford *Complete Works* of 1986 put this policy into practice, providing an abundance of editorial stage directions, quite possibly more than any earlier edition. To pick an example at random, the opening scene of *Romeo and Juliet* has no fewer than eighteen added or expanded stage directions, as opposed to seven in the Riverside or five in the Arden 2 edition. Arguably, Wells's project was not only to make 'the staging intelligible' but also, as he put it in a later essay, to try 'to realize the theatrical dimension of the text'.[150] Commenting on a specific dramatic situation in which editors can choose to add stage directions, he wrote: 'an editor who is trying to realize the theatrical dimension of the text owes it to his readers to indicate points for both kneeling and rising by means of stage directions'.[151] *Romeo and Juliet* in the Oxford *Complete Works* again allows us to see this policy in practice:

JULIET   (*kneeling*)
                 Good father, I beseech you on my knees,
                 Hear me with patience but to speak a word.

CAPULET
                 Hang thee, young baggage, disobedient wretch!
                 I tell thee what: get thee to church o' Thursday,
                 Or never after look me in the face.
                 Speak not, reply not, do not answer me.
                 [*Juliet rises*]
                 My fingers itch. Wife, we scarce thought us blest
                 That God had lent us but this only child,
                 But now I see this one is one too much,
                 And that we have a curse in having her.
                 Out on her, hilding!

                                                              (3.5.158–68)

The passage adds two stage directions to describe Juliet's movements. The moment she kneels down is suggested by the implied stage direction, 'I beseech you on my knees', but there is nothing in the text to suggest when she rises, and the moment chosen by the editors may seem surprising. Their solution is in interesting contrast with that adopted by Jill Levenson in the Oxford series. Instead of adding a stage direction to get Juliet back on her feet, Levenson comments in a footnote on the performance choices in actual productions: 'In most prompt books Juliet . . . remains on the ground . . . for much of the exchange which follows.' While the Oxford *Complete Works* make Juliet rise only five lines after she knelt down, most productions seem to do so considerably later. It is possible to speculate about the reasons for the respective choices. If Juliet kneels down in order to sway her father's opinion, his harshly intransigent answer in the first three lines of his speech make it clear that he will not change his mind, and the reason for her kneeling being thus obsolete, she can be made to rise again. Directors and actresses, by contrast, may have felt that, no matter what the pragmatic purpose of Juliet's kneeling is, the crushing response with which her plea is met puts her in a psychological disposition that does not make her rise but, if anything, fall flat on the ground, crying, as Romeo does in 3.3, which may well be meant to rhyme visually with the expression of Juliet's grief in 3.5. So does the passage illustrate Braunmuller's point that 'persons equipped to make good editions of old plays are . . . rarely equipped (or at best only intermittently equipped) to understand matters of performance to the same standard'?[152]

More importantly, the example serves to exemplify the differences between prescriptive editorial stage directions and descriptive commentary notes, the two chief alternatives in the editorial mediation of stage action. Some editors, as pointed out above, add a stage direction to suggest that Polonius's words 'Take this from this if this be otherwise' are accompanied by him '*touching his head, then his shoulder*'. Yet other editors do not, preferring instead to explain the options in the commentary: 'Theobald thought Polonius pointed to his head and shoulders. Dowden suggested he meant taking his wand of office from his hand' (New Cambridge); 'Polonius gestures to his head and his shoulder (or to his chain of office and his neck, or to his staff of office and his hand), indicating that he would yield up his life (or his office) if proved wrong' (Folger). Similarly, while some editions import Q1's stage direction into their Q2-based text to suggest that when Romeo '*offers to stab himself*', the '*Nurse snatches the dagger away*', other editors do not, but instead explain, as Levenson does, that in some productions, Friar Laurence intervenes, but that others follow Q1 in having the Nurse do so.

The scholarly debate outlined above about the best way of editorially mediating stage action reveals a clash of two editorial imperatives: facilitating and disambiguating understanding by explaining in the text what happens and when things happen (which an editor can do by adding prescriptive stage directions), or preserving the text's performative potential (which an editor can do by refraining from adding prescriptive stage directions and instead commenting on the options in the commentary). What should be the editor's priority in the mediation of stage action: intelligibility (at the risk of confining alternatives to footnotes which 'nobody reads') or variability (at the risk of confining the mention of stage action to those same neglected footnotes)? As the preceding paragraphs indicate, the answer to this question, important though its repercussions are, is not one on which well-informed scholars are likely to agree any time soon.

In recent years, there have been attempts to go beyond the limitations of prescriptive stage directions or descriptive commentary notes. Arguing that we need to 'reintroduce variability . . . into our understanding of the relationship between dramatic text and performance',[153] Kidnie has addressed the question of 'how we might translate the stage directions of early modern scripts in such a way as to make readers aware of textual indeterminacy'.[154] She shows that we might do so by 'experimenting more freely with the layout of the edited page'.[155] Presenting the text in two adjacent vertical boxes, a broad box on the right with the dialogue text and a narrow box to the left with stage directions, Kidnie provides sample passages in which stage directions appear alongside the dialogue text rather than at a specific moment within it, 'delimiting a probable range' within which stage action happens and suggesting the simultaneity of stage action and dialogue.[156] A related presentational novelty has been adopted by Bate and Rasmussen. Like Kidnie, they reserve a separate column for stage directions, though they place the column to the right of the dialogue text and reserve it for *editorial* stage directions, keeping *original* stage directions in the main body of the text. What their solution shares with Kidnie's presentational device is that, while not confining the editorial mediation of stage action to the commentary (thereby preserving its privileged visibility), it does not conflate the editor's stage directions and the original dialogue text but keeps them visibly apart. Therefore, the separate space the stage directions occupy highlights their status as a site of editorial intervention.

As Walter Ong has argued, any critical writing we undertake implies fictionalizing a readership.[157] This also applies to the making of a critical edition. There is a crucial difference between how the editions advocated by Wells, Williams, and Foakes fictionalize their readers and how Kidnie and Cox's do so. The former conceptualize them as spectators of a performance imagined by the editor, while the latter see them as directors of the mind who interact with the text's performative potential. By eschewing directorial editing, the latter invite readers to engage with the text's instability. By embedding editorial stage directions in the text, the former facilitate understanding and decisively shape how readers imagine performance, but they do so at the risk of foreclosing the performance potential inherent in the play text.

The chief question I have been grappling with above is *how* readers are best made aware of the stage action implied by the dialogue, or, to put this differently, *how* editors best enable them to visualize the stage action. The question I now wish to turn to is *what* readers should be made to visualize: the represented fiction or the theatrical representation? The issue goes to the heart of what exactly it is we do when we read a play. The histrionic activity designated by the word 'play' implies a stage, or some other playing space, where the play is performed. Yet as students of literature, we read dramatic texts and engage with them on the page. As we do so, should we be encouraged by editors to imagine, say, the Forest of Arden and the castle of Elsinore *or* the theatrical space in which these places are set? Should we imagine, to put it in the words of the Prologue in *Henry V*, the 'vasty fields of France' or the 'wooden O'?

It is interesting to observe that the answers editors give to these questions changed in the course of the twentieth century. The opening stage direction of John Dover Wilson's edition of *Richard II* may serve to illustrate how they changed: 'A great scaffold within the castle at Windsor, with seats thereon, and a space of ground before it. "Enter King Richard, John of Gaunt, with the Duke of Surrey, other nobles and attendants." They ascend the scaffold and sit in their places, the King in a chair of justice in the midst.' By contrast, the opening stage direction in the first edition of 1597, from which Wilson's edition had been set up, reads: 'ENTER KING RICHARD, IOHN OF GAVNT, WITH OTHER *Nobles and attendants*' (Q1, A2r). Wilson's expanded opening direction shows that his edition is fictional rather than theatrical, encouraging the reader to imagine the King in the castle at Windsor rather than on a stage. Other examples are similarly telling. A stage direction added to Wilson and Arthur Quiller-Couch's edition of *A Midsummer Night's Dream* reads: 'The air is heavy with the scent of blossom'

(2.2.0). Wilson's edition of *Richard II* was published in 1939, and his and Quiller-Couch's *Midsummer Night's Dream* appeared as early as 1924. No recent edition of these plays adopts their fictional stage directions.

Another way of observing the move from one convention to another in the course of the twentieth century is to trace the gradual disappearance of the indications of locality (a room in a castle, the heath, a courtroom in Venice) with which scenes had long been preceded, all the way back to Alexander Pope in the early eighteenth century.[158] They are still found in the Cambridge series dating from the early decades of the century, but they have disappeared in the *New* Cambridge series which has been appearing since the 1980s (though some editors continue to provide indications in footnotes). Peter Alexander's *Complete Works* of 1951 still has them, but more recent complete works like the Oxford, the Norton, or the Riverside no longer do. The Craig/Bevington *Complete Works* of 1973 still print the location in the text, but the more recent Bevington *Complete Works* confine them to footnotes. The Arden 1 series from early in the twentieth century still has indications of locality, but Arden 3 which is currently in progress no longer does. Their disappearance from the main text can in fact be observed in the course of the Arden 2 series, with some editions still containing them (like *Measure for Measure* of 1965) at a time when others had already dispensed with them (for instance *The Winter's Tale*, published in 1963). So editions up to the 1960s tended to encourage a readerly reception that imagined the space as it is represented in the play, while more recent practice encourages us to imagine the space in which the play would have been performed.

This recent practice has been theoried by Stanley Wells. Arguing that 'the editor needs to identify points at which additional directions, or changes to those of the early texts, are necessary to make the staging intelligible', he adds: 'Needless to say . . . the editor has to think in terms of the Elizabethan stage. No serious editor, I suppose, would disagree with this.'[159] Accordingly, added stage directions in recent editions typically assume a performance space modelled on the Elizabethan playhouses with, for instance, a space above (the gallery over the stage), a main stage below, a space within (the tiring house from which certain characters speak or make noise), and a discovery space. So in the Oxford *Complete Works*, to give a few examples, the editors decided that the ghosts in *Richard III* enter '*above*' (5.5.70). In *Troilus and Cressida*, Cressida similarly enters '*above*', whereas Aeneas, Antenor, Hector, Paris, Helenus, and Troilus pass by '*below*' (1.2.1–222). Later in the same play, '*One knocks within*' (4.2.42), as there is '*A noise within*' in *Measure for Measure* (1.2.103). In *Measure for Measure*, at the beginning of 4.1, Mariana does not enter but is '*discovered*'. In *Timon of Athens*, the Oxford editors add stage directions according to which '*Mercer passes over the stage*' and '*The Senators pass over the stage*' (1.1.7, 41). Many more examples could be given, but the point, I think, has been made: the added stage directions are firmly embedded in a stage, more precisely in an Elizabethan stage, and what the reader is made to visualize is thus the theatrical representation, not the represented dramatic fiction.

Yet is it really 'needless to say', as Wells believes, that added stage directions should be modelled upon what we know about the Elizabethan stage? After all, as Kidnie has incisively argued, since most of the evidence of early modern stagings is lost, the Oxford editors' intervention, although it claims to proceed by reference to the Elizabethan stage, is inevitably modern rather than early modern: 'it is a mistake to assume that the staging we currently lack would seem familiar or natural to us, in keeping, that is, with our own contemporary theatrical expectations. Instead of regarding interventionist editing of staging as a means by which the reader gains a richer understanding of the play in performance, it is therefore more accurate to interpret this particular editorial function as a process by which the script is systematically shaped to create for the reader a specifically modern and, for this reason, accessible virtual performance'.[160]

Even more fundamentally, we may query why editorial stage directions should necessarily contribute to making the reader visualize the theatrical representation, not the represented dramatic fiction. Wells takes it 'as axiomatic that the plays take place, not on heaths, in forests, in castles, in palaces, in ante-rooms, or bedrooms, or throne-rooms, but on a stage'.[161] Yet this, it seems to me, is mistaking one medium for another, the performed play for the printed play text. It is true that Shakespeare's plays were written to be performed on stage, but it is also true that they were printed to be read on the page. Shakespeare's plays have always led an existence in two media, and collapsing their peculiarities arguably does justice to neither. What undeniably takes place on a stage is a theatrical performance of, say, *Macbeth*, but a reading of *Macbeth* takes place, if anywhere, in the reader's mind. What the reader is made to imagine, *Macbeth* on stage or *Macbeth* in Scotland, is something which editorial policy can partly shape, and not a commonsensical given, as Wells would have us believe.

What seems to underlie Wells's view is that a dramatic text is somehow incomplete until it is performed and that the best editors can therefore do is to turn the playtext into a surrogate performance. Yet while it is possible to see a playtext as a theatrical script, it is by no means necessary to do so. Indeed, as Kidnie has put it, 'There is no necessary link between dramatic literature and the stage'.[162] Stephen Orgel has recently added that 'those readers for whom the text is not a surrogate performance but a book . . . probably have always constituted most of the market for published plays'.[163]

It may be argued that the kind of added stage directions with which readers are made to visualize the theatrical representation instead of the represented fiction, the stage rather than the Castle of Inverness, can also be found in the playbooks printed in Shakespeare's own time, not only in modern editions. For instance, in the First Quarto of *The Merchant of Venice*, Jessica enters '*aboue*' (D2r, 2.6.26), and Brabantio, in the First Folio edition of *Othello*, does the same (TLN 89, 1.1.83). A number of characters can be heard from '*within*'. The Ghost in *Hamlet* '*cries under the Stage*' (Q2, D4v, 1.5.158), in *Antony and Cleopatra*, '*Musicke of the Hoboyes is vnder the Stage*' (TLN 2482, 4.3.12); and in the First Folio edition of *3 Henry VI*, '*Richard and Hastings flyes ouer the Stage*' (TLN 2258–59, 4.3.27). It would be difficult to deny that in these instances, the original directions encourage us to locate the action on the stage.

Yet while Shakespeare's early modern playbooks do contain *theatrical* stage directions, it is no less true that they also contain *fictional* stage directions. A number of characters do not simply enter 'above' but in locations which clearly function as the fictional equivalent. In the First Quarto of *Richard II*, the King '*appeareth on the walls*' (F4v, 3.3.61); *Coriolanus* mentions '*two Senators with others on the Walles of Corialus*' (TLN 499–500, 1.4.13); in Folio *3 Henry VI*, the Mayor of York and his brethren '*Enter on the Walls*' (TLN 2511, 4.7.16), and later in the same play King Henry and Richard, Duke of Gloucester, are also '*on the Walles*' (TLN 3073, 5.6.0), as is a '*Citizen*' in *King John* (TLN 505, 2.1.200). Other characters appear at a window, and since there is 'no reliable external evidence of actual *windows* on the upper level this is best considered a *fictional* term for a dialogue-created location'.[164] In the First Quarto of *Othello*, Brabantio appears '*at a window*' (B2r); in *The Taming of the Shrew*, the '*Pedant lookes out of the window*' (TLN 2397, 5.1.15); and in *Henry VIII*, the King and Butts appear '*at a Windowe aboue*' (TLN 3014–15, 5.2.19). Perhaps most unusually, Lord Scales, in *2 Henry VI*, enters '*upon the Tower walking*' (TLN 2598, 4.5.0). In all these instances, the actors would have appeared in the gallery above the main stage, but the stage directions instead refer to the fictional locations for which the gallery stood.

Similarly, while many characters enter at a (theatrical) 'door', others, in keeping with the dramatic fiction, '*Enter to the gates*' (*King John*, TLN 608–9, 2.1.299) or '*enter the City*' (*Coriolanus*, TLN 568, 1.4.67). Folio *Henry V* has '*the King and all his Traine before the Gates*' (TLN 1259, 3.3.0), and in *Coriolanus*, Martius '*follows them* [the Volsces] *to gates, and is shut in*' (TLN 538–9, 1.4.43). While noise can simply come from 'within', Folio *2 Henry VI* describes its origins in terms of the dramatic fiction: '*Alarum. Fight at Sea. Ordnance goes off*' (TLN 2168, 4.1.0). The trapdoor was the theatrical location into which characters could descend, but Folio *Hamlet* describes use of the trapdoor again in fictional terms when the protagonist '*Leaps in the graue*' (TLN 3444, 5.1.250). Similarly, Ariel '*vanishes in Thunder*' (*The Tempest*, TLN 1616, 3.3.82), clearly 'a sudden departure through a *trapdoor*',[165] expressed in fictional rather than theatrical terms. Many more instances of fictional stage directions could be added: '*Enter Pericles a* [on] *Shipboard*' (Q1 *Pericles*, E1v, 3.1.0); '*Enter Brutus in his Orchard*' (*Julius Caesar*, TLN 615, 2.1.0); '*the Romans are beat back to their Trenches*' (*Coriolanus*, TLN 523, 1.4.30); '*Enter Belarius, Guiderius, Aruiragus, and Imogen from the Caue*' (*Cymbeline*, TLN 2244–5, 4.2.0); '*Enter Timon out of his Caue*' (*Timon of Athens*, TLN 2360, 5.1.129). On countless occasions, the original stage directions in Shakespeare's playtexts cause a reader to visualize the represented fiction and not the theatrical representation.

In their *Dictionary of Stage Directions in English Drama, 1580–1642*, Alan C. Dessen and Leslie Thomson record a great number of what they call 'fictional terms directed at a reader'.[166] As they make clear, Shakespeare is one among several dramatists who repeatedly uses 'fictional directions' which conform to 'a narrative, descriptive style seemingly more suited to a reader facing a page than an actor on the stage'.[167] As their useful distinction (borrowed from Richard Hosley) between theatrical and fictional stage directions makes clear, Shakespeare made extensive use of both kinds. This bifold use reflects the double reception Shakespeare knew his plays were receiving: on the one hand, his texts functioned as theatrical scripts which he and his fellow actors transformed in preparing the plays for the stage; on the other hand, his texts were printed and reprinted, collected and bound, read and excerpted, like those of no other dramatist. Therefore, it should not surprise us that Shakespeare directs his stage directions partly at his fellow actors by locating the action within their theatrical structure and partly at his readers 'facing a page'.

What the abundance of fictional stage directions in Shakespeare's original playtexts makes clear is that there is no reason why modern editors, when adding more directions with the aim of helping readers visualize the action, should refrain from doing what Shakespeare did. Wells takes it 'as axiomatic that the plays take place . . . on a stage',[168] but if stage directions in Shakespeare's original playtexts suggest that they also take place in fictional locations, Shakespeare's modern editors may want to suggest the same. We can be glad that Dover Wilson has no followers among modern editors: his stage directions were irresponsibly imaginative, no more than loosely tied, at best, to the original text. Yet while Dover Wilson's specific practice was flawed, the mere idea of editorially anchoring the action in the dramatic fiction rather than the stage is a legitimate possibility. As Kidnie put it, 'characters at one time entered anterooms in Scottish castles, now they simply enter the scene. . . . These adjustments . . . are evidence of ever-changing fashions in the way stage directions are adapted to modern sensibilities and conventions'.[169] The still dominant conventions conform to the imperatives of performance criticism, which, in the last decades of the twentieth century, constituted a welcome reaction to the New Critical, text-centred approach it superseded. Yet just as critical approaches underwent profound changes in the twentieth century, they will continue to do so in the twenty-first century. In particular, the current re-evaluation of Shakespeare's authorial standing may well be leading to a critical climate in which it will be easier to do justice to Shakespeare's dramatic fiction than it was at the end of the last century.

Before concluding this chapter, I wish to test the idea that plays may take place in fictional space rather than solely on a stage. In a recent essay, called 'The Book of the Play', Stephen Orgel has investigated the relationship between the printed playtexts and the stage by means of woodcut illustrations in playbooks by Shakespeare's contemporaries: 'For plays, English publishers from the 1590s on occasionally provided, as a frontispiece or on the title-page, a scene from the play.' As a close look at these woodcuts reveals, 'The sources of this kind of representation are images that, however dramatic, have no connection with plays or theater ... nothing here suggests a theater'.[170] Concerning the famous illustration of the 1615 edition of Thomas Kyd's *The Spanish Tragedy*, for instance, it has been shown that 'The illustration as a whole may have no direct connection with stage performances, and certainly no attempt has been made in it to suggest a stage'.[171] The woodcut for Francis Beaumont and John Fletcher's *A King and No King* is 'set in a fanciful hilly landscape', and so is the one for the same authors' *The Maid's Tragedy*.[172] Noting how the woodcuts detach the play's action from the stage, Orgel asks, 'What do readers want out of plays?', and goes on to suggest that what they want are 'Many and various things, clearly, most of which have nothing to do with theater'.[173] If this is true, then the earliest readers of Shakespeare's playbooks might have been surprised by the categorical assertion that 'plays take place ... on a stage'.

In this chapter, I have tried to show what is at stake in the modern editorial mediation of stage action. Owing to the scarcity and imprecision of stage directions in Shakespeare's early playbooks, modern editors have the considerable responsibility of spelling out what action can be inferred from the text. By doing so, most editors add to the original text, complementing Shakespeare's words with their own, collaborating with Shakespeare so as to make the text as intelligible as possible. How exactly this process is best undertaken is, I have suggested, a complex question to which several intellectually defensible answers can and have been given. In particular, scholars disagree on *how* an editor best enables readers to visualize the stage action: by embedding a single choice in the text or by alerting readers to the range of staging possibilities by refusing to do so. Furthermore, I have argued that the editor's responsibility is also to decide *what* the reader is enabled to visualize: the staged theatrical representation or the represented dramatic fiction. Editors decide how we readers imagine the action in Shakespeare's plays.

4 Editing the Real *Lear*

The preceding chapter focuses on a single issue: the modern editorial mediation of Shakespeare; the present chapter concentrates on a single play: *King Lear*. The problems raised by Chapter 3 are of a pragmatic nature: what is an editor to do about the scarcity of stage directions in Shakespeare's early playbooks? The more fundamental editorial problem underlying Chapter 4 is ontological: what *is King Lear*? It was long taken for granted that we know what constitutes the play called *King Lear*, but it seems no longer clear whether we really do. For much of the twentieth century, scholars maintained that the real *King Lear* had disappeared from the English stage soon after the Restoration when Nahum Tate reworked the play in 1681. Tate's version omitted some 800 lines, got rid of the Fool and the King of France, famously added a love relationship between Edgar and Cordelia, and ended happily by preserving the lives of Kent, Gloucester, Cordelia, and Lear. The standard view therefore was that the real *Lear* only returned to the stage in 1838 when William Charles Macready produced the play in its original form. However, more recently, other scholars have started arguing that the *King Lear* that was read and performed for much of the nineteenth and twentieth centuries was not the real play after all but that it was in fact a conflation of two *Lear*s, identical with neither and thus not the real *Lear*. Since the two-*Lear* argument has gained in prominence, it has become clear that the question of what the real *Lear* is persists. Indeed, it seems legitimate to ask whether it is by accident that 'real' is an anagram of 'Lear'.

The first of the two *Lear*s was published in 1608, in quarto format, with the following title: 'M. William Shak-speare: HIS True Chronicle Historie of the life and death of King LEAR and his three Daughters. *With the vnfortunate life of* Edgar, *sonne* and heire to the Earle of Gloster, and his sullen and assumed humor of TOM of Bedlam'. The Second Quarto of 1619 is essentially a reprint, but in 1623, a different *King Lear* appeared in the First Folio, called, more concisely, 'THE TRAGEDIE OF KING LEAR'. The 1608 *History of King Lear* is approximately 3,100 lines long, while the 1623 *Tragedy of King Lear* amounts to about 2,900 lines. The *History* contains some 300 lines which are absent from the *Tragedy*, while the *Tragedy* has about 100 lines that are not in the *History*. In particular, the 'mock trial' (3.6) with mad Lear's denunciation of Regan and Goneril is only in the Quarto, as are a number of passages alluding to the presence of the French army in England. In addition, of the lines that are present in both texts, a small number are attributed to different speakers. For instance, Albany speaks the crucial final lines in the Quarto, Edgar in the Folio.

Long before the two-*Lear* theory was advanced in the late twentieth century, scholars had been aware of the textual differences between the Quarto and the Folio, but the dominant explanation at the time effectively led to their editorial suppression. The *History* and the *Tragedy* were thought to reflect imperfectly a perfect Shakespearean original, an original which had been distorted in the playhouse or in the printing house. Lewis Theobald argued as early as 1733 that there must have been one text of *King Lear*, and that corruption of Shakespeare's text was at the origin of the differences between the Quartos and the Folio.[174] Two and a half centuries later, this theory was challenged by scholars who argued that the differences between the two versions are not simply accidental but form part of a discernable pattern for which only Shakespeare himself can be held responsible. In other words, the revisionists held that Shakespeare revised *King Lear*, turning the original *History* into the later *Tragedy*.

The revisionists' earliest publications appeared in 1978[175] and 1980,[176] and by 1983, the movement had gained enough steam for a 500-page collection, *The Division of the Kingdoms*, to establish the case.[177] Yet other scholars remained sceptical. While the revisionists believed that, in order to account for Q/F differences, 'all that is needed is Shakespeare',[178] others held that the cuts made from the Quarto were likely to have been made by someone else[179] or that the Q/F differences do 'not necessarily form part of a systematic revision'.[180] The revisionists considered Folio *Lear* the result of skilful authorial revision which significantly improved the play; the sceptics saw in it no more than partly botched 'theatrical surgery' through which 'the play loses more than it gains'.[181] Whereas 'the two-text revolutionaries'[182] insisted on the essential difference between *The History* and *The Tragedy*, more moderate critics preferred to speak of 'two versions of the same play, not two different plays'.[183] On either side of the divide, theatrical arguments were used to bolster the case. While a revisionist argued that 'the major variants in *King Lear* are the result of careful revision performed by a theater artist, most probably by Shakespeare himself',[184] another scholar argued that the Folio constitutes no theatrical improvement.[185] The Folio omission of the trial scene similarly received diametrically opposed interpretations, resulting in a superior version according to one critic[186] and in an inferior version according to another.[187] In recent years, no consensus has been emerging, and one scholar has come to the conclusion that 'the theory of authorial revision seems to have receded to the only position it can reasonably achieve – that of an unverifiable hypothesis'.[188]

Even though the scholarly debate over the texts of *King Lear* has led to no certainties regarding their respective quality and the agency that accounts for their existence, it clearly has led to an increased awareness of the divergences between them. Some scholars rightly pointed out that these are local rather than pervasive, and that they are mostly a matter of omissions, additions, and reassignments, not of actual rewriting. Nevertheless, it is undeniable that the differences can have a significant impact on how readers interpret the play. Therefore, faced with the complex textual situation and the inconclusive debate in recent scholarship, editors of *King Lear* have momentous decisions to take. They decide, in effect, what many of their readers will consider the real *Lear*.

Before examining the decisions editors have taken or could take, I wish to examine the potential impact of these decisions by demonstrating what interpretative repercussions local Q/F differences can have. A good way of assessing these repercussions is to turn to the play's ending and to examine how Lear dies. The Folio *Tragedy* contains the text we are traditionally familiar with:

> *Lear.* And my poore Foole is hang'd: no, no, no life?
> Why should a Dog, a Horse, a Rat haue life,
> And thou no breath at all? Thou'lt come no more,
> Neuer, neuer, neuer, neuer, neuer.
> Pray you vndo this Button. Thanke you Sir,
> Do you see this? Looke on her? Looke her lips,
> Looke there, looke there.   *He dis.*

Lear's final speech is seven lines long. He laments Cordelia's death, then asks for a button to be undone. At the end of the speech, Lear has his attention fixed on Cordelia because, as most critics have argued, he mistakenly believes that she is coming back to life or is still alive: 'Do you see this? Looke on her? Looke her lips, / Looke there, looke there', followed by the stage direction, '*He di[e]s*' (TLN 3282–83). These words allow of course for different interpretati[189] but the dominant view since A. C. Bradley[190] is that Lear dies in a moment of extreme joy, contemplating his dead daughter, fancying that her lips are moving and that she is therefore alive.[191]

Yet in the Quarto *History*, the moment of Lear's death is dramatized very differently:

> *Lear.* And my poore foole is hangd: no, no life; why should a dog, a horse, a rat haue life, and thou no breath at all, O thou wilt come no more, neuer, neuer, neuer: pray you vndo this button, thanke you sir, O, o,o,o. *Edg.* He faints my Lord, my Lord.
> *Lear.* Breake hart, I prethe breake. *Edgar.* Look vp my Lord.

Here, the speech is only four lines long, not seven, and omits precisely the lines about Cordelia's lips. As in the Folio, Lear asks for a button to be opened. Following the words 'thanke you sir', all the Quarto adds are four 'O's, the agonizing sounds Lear is making shortly before his death. Yet he does not die immediately, as he does in the Folio, but speaks a few more words slightly later: 'Breake hart, I prethe breake' (L4r). The Folio has exactly the same words, but here they are attributed to Kent, not to Lear.

An obvious difference between Quarto and Folio is that the King in the Quarto dies while focusing on himself – 'Breake hart, I prethe breake' – while in the Folio, he dies seemingly unmindful of his own state, preoccupied solely with his daughter. Shakespeare's tragic heroes typically have a moment of self-consciousness before they die; Lear in the Quarto does so too, but Lear in the Folio does not. Lear's final moment in the Folio is complex insofar as he is often believed to die at a moment of ecstatic joy, but if he dies believing Cordelia to be alive, he also dies in ignorance of her true state, his ignorance forming a last ironic contrast with our own knowledge, a contrast that is of course important in the play as early as the first scene. Lear's death in the Quarto in some ways resembles Antony's death in *Antony and Cleopatra* where the protagonist similarly utters a death wish to himself: 'Oh, cleave, my sides! / Heart, once be stronger than thy continent; / Crack thy frail case' (4.14.39–41). This is similar to Lear in the Quarto, but not in the Folio. Even more importantly, in a play which derives considerable meaning from the relationship between main plot and subplot, Quarto Lear's death resembles – but Folio Lear's death does not resemble – that of Gloucester, whose heart 'burst smilingly' (5.3.203), according to Edgar's report. There is of course no sense in which awareness of the differences between the Quarto and the Folio texts can allow us privileged access to some kind of essential meaning of either or both texts. Either text, obviously, can be interpreted in a variety of ways, but it seems fair to say that the Quarto and the Folio's dramatization of Lear's death differ significantly.

Another notable Q/F difference in these lines is that the Folio regularizes the speech as it appears in the Quarto. In the Quarto's five-line speech, the first line is a syllable short and the third line two syllables long, a hexameter, not a pentameter. In the Folio, by contrast, before the final line, which appropriately stops half way through at the moment Lear dies, the six preceding lines are all decasyllables and conform readily enough to a five-stress pattern. Since Shakespeare's verse is by no means always regular, recent scholarship warns us against doubting the authority of the Quarto text simply because it has fewer iambic pentameters than the Folio.

The dramatization of Lear's death is a crucial feature of the differences between the ending of the two versions, but other elements of this passage also require attention. The speech's first words have a particularly complex resonance: 'And my poor fool is hanged' (5.3.311). Lear seems to be referring to Cordelia, yet the affectionate word he uses to designate his daughter, 'fool', simultaneously calls up the play's real Fool who was with Lear for much of the first three acts before disappearing from the play for no apparent reason. It seems clear that Shakespeare mustered what poetic means there are to draw attention to the words 'poor fool'. The two words are not only linked to each other by assonance but they also constitute a spondaic foot. Even though Shakespeare rarely indulges in this kind of typographic pun, we may even speculate whether the final four 'O's take up and mirror the four 'o's in 'poor fool' at the beginning of the speech. However that may be, the words may suggest that Shakespeare, at the moment of Cordelia's death brought about by the play's villain, Edmund, chose to remind us of the Fool's disappearance, his dramatic death, as it were, brought about by Shakespeare himself. Shakespeare seems to trigger a momentary resurrection of the Fool in our consciousness before the play ends, not unlike Cordelia's coming back to life according to Lear's flawed consciousness. Yet it is important to notice that this complex resonance is not a feature of both texts but only of *The Tragedy of King Lear*.

The differences in Lear's final speech also affect the interpretation of the passage that precedes it. In both texts, Lear says: 'shees gone for euer. / I know when one is dead, and when one liues' (Q L3v, 5.3.264–65). In the Folio, though not in the Quarto, this passage is ironic in the light of Lear's final words. A few lines later, Lear, in his madness, goes on to undermine what he has just said, this time asserting that 'she lives! If it be so, / It is a chance which does redeem all sorrows / That ever I have felt' (5.2.270–72). Again, the lines are highly significant in the light of the Folio ending where Lear seems to die believing that Cordelia is indeed alive. Lear is using the highly charged word 'redeem', saying that this 'chance' (meaning 'outcome') 'redeems' (in the sense of 'making up for') all the sorrows he has been experiencing (OED, v.1). Yet uttered by a character who is about to die, the word, in an intensely Christian seventeenth-century context, at the same time calls up another meaning of 'redeem', that of deliverance from sin and its consequences (OED, v.6). It is of course possible to argue that *Lear* is a play with a pagan setting from which Christianity is largely absent, but it may be responded that various passages, including Kent's allusion to the Apocalypse, 'Is this the promised end' (5.3.268), strengthen the anachronistic Christian overtones of the play's final moments.

Suffering and redemption are often paired within a Christian framework, and it seems possible to argue that the Folio *Tragedy of King Lear* brings the two together: Lear claims he will be 'redeemed' if Cordelia is alive shortly before dying in the belief that Cordelia is indeed alive. This juxtaposition does not exist in the Quarto, and the *History* therefore does not seem to evoke the possibility of a kind of redemption through Cordelia in order to remind us of that possibility at the moment of Lear's death. What may further complicate the question of Lear's 'redemption' is that Lear has just admitted that he has killed the person whom Edmund had ordered to hang Cordelia. To make sure we do not interpret Lear's words as another instance of his madness, Shakespeare has the Captain, who was sent in vain to save Cordelia, confirm Lear's words. 'I killed the slave that was a-hanging thee', Lear says. '"Tis true, my lords, he did' (5.3.279–80), the Captain confirms. Despite the pagan setting, Shakespeare, in the Folio version, may be *stressing* Lear's need for redemption as the play draws to its tragic close.

I have tried to illustrate the significant differences in the way the Quarto and the Folio dramatize the final moments leading up to Lear's death, differences with potentially far-reaching interpretative repercussions. I have been focusing on the differences in the dramatization of Lear's death, but a number of other aspects could have been highlighted in similar fashion. The assignment of the final speech in the Quarto to Albany but in the Folio to Edgar allows for a rather different interpretation of the play's final moment. The passages alluding to the French army in England which are absent from the Folio can lead to a rather different understanding of the play's politics. A number of passages added in one and omitted in the other text make of Edgar a more and of Kent a less important character in the Folio than in the Quarto. The Folio omits the short choric scene, usually Act 4, Scene 3 in traditional, conflated editions, in which a gentleman reports

Cordelia's tearful reaction to the news about her father. The *History* thus reveals a dimension of the character that is absent from the *Tragedy*, all the more so as the melodramatic portrait of Cordelia contrasts rather sharply with the determined leader of the French invasion in the following scene, Act 4, Scene 4.

In the light of the above examples, it seems difficult to deny that the differences between the *History* and the *Tragedy of King Lear* can have important critical repercussions, and those who ignore them risk being textually and critically naïve. In 1990, one of the foremost modern Shakespeare scholars wrote that Lear 'dies still looking on his daughter's lips for the words that she never speaks',[192] and a decade later, another leading scholar argued for the importance of the words 'see' and 'look' in the play, claiming that the latter word occurs 'four times in Lear's last ten words'.[193] These are correct statements about *The Tragedy* but not about *The History of King Lear*, as criticism with greater textual awareness would spell out.

Now that it has been established that the Quarto and the Folio editions of *King Lear* significantly differ (even though scholars will disagree as to why they do so), it seems important to ask what this means for editors of *King Lear*. What *King Lear*, or *King Lear*s, should they now mediate to readers? How should we now read *Lear* (an important issue, it seems to me, not simply an Anglo-French pun)? Should we now read one text rather than the other? If so, which one? Or should we study both at the same time? If so, how? Or should we continue reading conflations? If so, how should they be presented? Scholars who have been commissioned to edit *King Lear* need to provide answers to these questions. Intriguingly, since the revisionists argued their case in the late 1970s and the 1980s, every editor has come up with a different answer; every editor has in fact constructed a different *Lear*.

The first edition reflecting the new textual theory on *King Lear* was published in the Oxford *Complete Works* in 1986, under the general editorship of Stanley Wells and Gary Taylor. Taylor being among the scholars who had carried out the revisionist scholarship, it was clear that this edition would reflect its arguments. The solution Wells and Taylor adopted was to print both versions of *King Lear*, first the *History of King Lear* of 1608 followed by the *Tragedy of King Lear* of 1623, giving both versions equal billing. In the second edition of the Oxford *Complete Works* of 2005, both *History* and *Tragedy* are still present, yet they no longer follow each other immediately but occupy their respective place in the volume according to the conjectured composition dates: the *History* '(1605–6)' between *Othello* '(1603–4)' and *Timon of Athens* '(1606)'; the *Tragedy* '(1610)' between *The Winter's Tale* '(1609–10)' and *Cymbeline* '(1610–11)'. This arrangement is arguably an even more determined affirmation of the two-*Lear* theory: whereas the first edition suggests two versions of one play, the second edition implies two plays on a similar subject.

When, in the 1990s, Norton was preparing its *Complete Works of Shakespeare* under the general editorship of Stephen Greenblatt, it was decided that the text would be based on the Oxford *Complete Works*, though annotations and introductions were provided by the Norton editors. The Norton edition thus took over the two versions printed in the Oxford *Complete Works* but also added a third, conflated text. Contrary to the Oxford editors, Norton printed the *History* and the *Tragedy* not serially but in parallel, the *History* on the left hand side and the *Tragedy* on the right, followed by the conflation. Norton's proliferation of *Lear*s may seem odd in the light of the fact that Greenblatt had failed to distinguish between the *History* and the *Tragedy* in a study published in 1990.

Contrary to the multiple *Lear*s in the Oxford *Complete Works* and Norton, Riverside and Bevington are content with a single text. Arguing that 'it is unwise to omit the material cut from the Folio text, since we cannot be sure that Shakespeare would have shortened the text had there been no external constraints' and that 'the added material in the Folio is clearly his and belongs in his conception of the play', Bevington opts for a traditional conflation which, he adds, 'avoids cutting material that Shakespeare may well have regretted having to excise' (A-6). G. Blakemore Evans, in the Riverside edition, similarly resists the 'the two-*Lear* theory': arguing that it is 'grounded on subjective interpretations of the "facts"',[194] he bases his edition on the *Tragedy* but includes, between square brackets, passages unique to Q1.

The above editions offer the complete works in one volume which naturally limits the amount of paratext, but several single-volume *King Lear* editions with full scholarly apparatus have been published in the last fifteen years. In the New Cambridge series, Jay Halio's *The Tragedy of King Lear* was published in 1992, based on the Folio. Two years later, the same editor published a second edition in the 'The Early Quartos' subseries, called *The First Quarto of King Lear*, based on the *History*. While the edition of the *Tragedy* comes with a full scholarly apparatus, introduction, stage history, annotation, and collation, the edition of the *First Quarto* has a simpler and exclusively textual apparatus: a textual introduction, textual notes, and collation. The New Cambridge thus establishes a hierarchy, the *Tragedy* belonging to the fully edited main series, while the *History* is confined to the more lightly edited subseries.

The Oxford Shakespeare series has adopted a simpler solution: published in 2001, *The History of King Lear: The 1608 Quarto*, edited by Stanley Wells, is strictly based on the First Quarto. No other *King Lear* edition seems to be planned in the series. Conversely, Bate and Rasmussen, in their Folio-based edition of the complete works, provide the text of *The Tragedy of King Lear* and add Q-only passages in an appendix. Arden 3 also confines itself to one edition, simply called '*King Lear*', edited by R. A. Foakes and published in 1997. This is a conflated edition, including all the passages that appear in only one of the two texts. In this, it resembles traditional conflations, but it departs from them by marking with small superscript Qs and Fs passages that are exclusive to one text, thus making visible the conflation in the main text instead of providing the information in the collation. In Arden 3, Lear's final speech looks like this:

LEAR
    And my poor fool is hanged. No, no, ᶠnoᶠ life!
    Why should a dog, a horse, a rat have life
    And thou no breath at all? ᵠOᵠ thou'lt come no more,
    Never, never, never, ᶠnever, never.ᶠ
    [*to Edgar?*] Pray you undo this button. Thank you, sir.
    ᵠO, o, o, o.ᵠ
    ᶠDo you see this? Look on her: look, her lips,
    Look there, look there!   *He dies.*ᶠ

In the first line, Lear repeats 'no' once in the Quarto but twice in the Folio, and in the fourth line he speaks 'never' five times as opposed to three times in the Quarto, so the last 'no' and the last two 'never's are marked between superscript Fs. Quarto Lear, contrary to Folio Lear, utters 'O' once in the third line and four more times two lines later, so these passages are marked between superscript Qs. The final two lines in the Folio, absent from the Quarto, are again between superscript Fs. The Arden 3 edition is thus old-style insofar as it conflates but new-style in that it stages the differences between the two texts.

The Folger edition similarly provides one text and uses typographic signs to highlight textual provenance, marking words which are Q1-only between pointed brackets and Folio-only lines between square brackets. Yet contrary to Arden 3, it only includes words and passages unique to Q1 when the editors consider them necessary. The text is based on the Folio, with Q1-only words added 'when their omission seems to leave a gap'.[195] On the other hand, 'when F lacks Q1 words that appear to add nothing of significance', the editors 'do not add these words'[196] to the text. The edition can thus be called a partial conflation with 'necessary' Q1 words added but 'needless' passages omitted.

In addition, two scholarly *King Lear* editions have been published that are not part of a Shakespeare series. Longman's 1993 *King Lear: A Parallel Text Edition*, prepared by René Weis, prints modernized texts of the *History* on the left and the *Tragedy* on the right hand side, and provides a full textual introduction and annotation. Finally, *The Complete King Lear*, edited by Michael Warren, was published by the University of California Press in 1989, undoubtedly one of the most innovative Shakespeare editions of the twentieth century. Warren provides a parallel-text of photographic facsimiles of the 1608 *History* and the 1623 *Tragedy*. In order to facilitate comparison, Warren has placed corresponding lines next to each other, one speech after the other, with white spaces in-between. In addition to this cut-and-paste facsimile parallel-text edition, Warren provides separate facsimile editions not only of the First Quarto and the First Folio versions but also of the Second Quarto, printed in 1619, which, even though it basically follows the First Quarto, introduces some local changes. The facsimiles of the three earliest editions do not come in codex format but consist of unbound fascicles, loose pieces of paper, one per page, allowing readers to use the edition any way they like, by reading one text sequentially or by putting next to each other the corresponding passages of more than one text. Warren's *Complete King Lear* genuinely tests the limits of what a print edition can do.[197]

The summary of this survey of scholarly *King Lear*s published in the last twenty-five years goes like this: one, the *History* and the *Tragedy* printed serially between the same covers; two, the *History* in parallel-text with the *Tragedy*, followed by a conflation, also between the same covers; three, separate volumes of the fully edited *Tragedy* in the main series and the more lightly edited *History* in a subseries; four, the Quarto-based *History of King Lear*, period; five, the Folio based *Tragedy* with Q-only passages in an appendix; six, a traditional conflation with all passages from the *History* and the *Tragedy* in one text; seven, a conflation with Q1-only passages between square brackets; eight, a conflation with superscript Qs and Fs marking the textual differences; nine, a partial conflation with F-only lines between square brackets, 'necessary' Q1-only passages included between pointed brackets, but 'needless' Q1-only material omitted; ten, a parallel-text *King Lear* with the *History* on the left and the *Tragedy* on the right; and eleven, *The Complete King Lear* with a parallel-text facsimile edition of *History* and *Tragedy* along with facsimile editions of the First Quarto, the Second Quarto and the Folio, in loose fascicles. Will the real *Lear* please stand up?

Nor is *King Lear* a unique case: among other two-text plays are *Troilus and Cressida*, *2 Henry IV*, and *Othello*. There are even three substantive texts of *Hamlet*, and the last quarter century shows a plethora of radically different editions. In 1982, Harold Jenkins's Arden 2 edition constituted the culmination of a long tradition of conflations. It intended 'to present the play as Shakespeare wrote it',[198] was chiefly based on the Second Quarto of 1604/5, but also liberally drew on the First Folio. (Q2 is the longest of the three substantive texts; F is slightly shorter, contains fewer than 100 lines absent from Q2 but lacks over 200 present in Q2; and Q1 (1603) is only just over half the length of Q2.) Two years later, Philip Edwards's *Hamlet* in the New Cambridge series was similarly eclectic but took a first step in helping readers distinguish between the different texts by printing passages confined to Q2 between square brackets. This device was developed in the Folger edition (1992), which marks between pointed brackets passages in F but not in Q2, and between square brackets passages in Q2 but not in the Folio. G. R. Hibbard based his Oxford edition (1987) on the Folio, as did the Oxford *Complete Works* (1986), confining Q2-

only passages to an appendix. They later regretted this decision, writing that 'It now seems obvious that we should have included two versions of *Hamlet*, as we did of *King Lear*, a Folio-based version and one based on Q2',[199] though they seem to have forgotten about their regrets by the time they prepared the second edition of the *Complete Works* (2005), to which they added editions of *Edward III* and *Sir Thomas More* but not of Q2 *Hamlet*. The inclusion of more than one version of *Hamlet* was put into practice in Paul Bertram and Bernice W. Kliman's *Three-Text Hamlet* (1990; 2nd ed. 2003), which places next to each other the corresponding passages of Q1, Q2, and F. Kliman also developed *The Enfolded Hamlet* (www.hamletworks.org), an electronic edition which highlights Q2/F differences by inserting Q2-only elements between curly brackets and in green, and F-only elements between pointed brackets and in pink. Jesús Tronch-Pérez's *Synoptic Hamlet: A Critical-Synoptic Edition of the Second Quarto and First Folio Texts of Hamlet* (2002) also makes available Q2/F variants in the text but does so by placing Q2 readings slightly above and F readings slightly below the line. Finally, the Arden 3 *Hamlet*, edited by Ann Thompson and Neil Taylor, provides separate editions of the three texts, the edition of Q2 occupying the core volume, with Q1 and F published jointly in a companion volume. As in the case of *Lear*, the recent multiplication of different *Hamlet*s raises the question of what constitutes Shakespeare's play. Indeed, a few generations ago, the question that haunted the reception of the play was: who is Hamlet? Today, by contrast, the question of greatest urgency seems to have become: what is *Hamlet*?

In less than twenty-five years, scholarly editors have produced more than ten radically different *Lear*s and a similar number of *Hamlet*s. Every recent editor has been mediating *King Lear* to readers in ways which are essentially different. If we recall what interpretative repercussions some of the Q/F differences have, we realize that it simply does not make sense to speak of *King Lear*, only of Foakes's *Lear*, Weis's *Lear*, or Halio's *Lear*. In a very real sense, the real *Lear* no longer exists but has given way to the editor's *Lear*. Similarly, the question of what *Hamlet* is depends on who the editor is. The recent editorial history of *King Lear* and *Hamlet* thus makes particularly clear that modern editions are in important ways collaborative constructions on which the editor has a crucial impact.

Conclusion

How many editions of Shakespeare do we need? A recent study contains a far from exhaustive list of more than 1,700 Shakespeare editions produced between the late sixteenth and the early twenty-first century. Of these editions, almost a thousand have been published since the beginning of the twentieth century.[200] As pointed out above, the last twenty-five years have witnessed the publication of more than ten important editions of *King Lear*. Other popular plays such as *Hamlet*, *Othello*, *Romeo and Juliet*, or *Henry V* total a similar number of editions in the same period of time, without counting further editions with no scholarly ambitions. Do we need more editions of Shakespeare's plays? This book suggests that we do. Shakespeare's playtexts do not simply exist out there, once and for all, but are always produced in the here and now. They may rightly be called textual performances, making the plays new, as theatrical performances make them new on stage. The preceding chapters have demonstrated that manifold operations go into the making of a scholarly edition, operations which are often of considerable complexity and continue to be subject to change in accordance with developments in textual thinking. Rather than providing us simply with more of the same, modern editors produce the Shakespeare of our time.

The editorial reproduction of Shakespeare's texts will thus continue, and continue to evolve. Future editors may well respond to the recent call for greater experimentation with the layout of the edited page, and find novel ways of encouraging 'imaginative interaction with the drama'.[201] Introductions, in particular, will be subject to change and continue to reflect shifts in critical fashions and scholarly paradigms. To venture only one prediction, few editions today provide a separate section in the introduction devoted to the play's history on screen, though it seems distinctly possible that such a section will become a standard feature of future editions. While the texts and paratexts in Shakespeare editions will undergo manifold changes, we can also hope that the future will see the publication of kinds of editions which are unavailable today. For instance, *Othello*, *Troilus and Cressida*, *2 Henry IV*, *Henry V*, and *Romeo and Juliet* are all multiple-play texts – like *King Lear* and *Hamlet* – but for none of them is a parallel-text edition in print. Other specialized editions are likely to come into being. The recent 'Shakespeare in Production' series, published by Cambridge University Press, offers annotation that confines itself to performance decisions in past productions. Performance criticism is currently in fashion, whereas source studies are not, but it is conceivable that, once the pendulum has swung back, there will be editions whose commentary will record in detail how Shakespeare transformed the source material he used.

Furthermore, it seems certain that digital editions will, in due course, significantly add to the current wealth of editions in print. Ongoing projects such as the Internet Shakespeare Edition (ise.uvic.ca, gen. ed. Michael Best) and hamletworks.org (gen. ed. Bernice W. Kliman) reveal some of the potential electronic editions have. In print, pressure on space is usually high; in the digital medium, it is not. Hyperlinks can establish connections that situate the text amidst a wealth of relevant intertexts. Revised editions of printed texts are expensive and require considerable effort, whereas electronic editions can easily be modified and added to. Print editions can have an index or indexes, and, with the help of print concordances, all occurrences of words can be located; yet digital editions can be searched with far greater ease and speed. Some of the advantages of the digital medium over print are so obvious that the best digital editions of the future will undoubtedly become a part of what edited Shakespeare can do for us.

This does not mean, as John Lavagnino has pointed out, that we will soon 'read everything online while our books collect dust'.[202] On the contrary, the codex is proving a remarkably resilient format for Shakespeare's texts. Whereas digital editions can be superior in some ways, print editions will remain more convenient in others. As Lavagnino has shown, for as simple a feature as annotation, the electronic edition cannot rival the convenience of the footnote at the bottom of the printed page.[203] It is therefore not surprising that the rate at which important editions have been appearing in print format shows no sign of slackening.

The editing of Shakespeare is usually entrusted to established scholars, and it is their editions, published by prestigious publishing houses and sold to thousands of users around the globe, that I have been examining in these pages. However, I have written this short book in the conviction – arrived at through classroom practice – that students have much to gain from their own hands-on editorial experience, an exercise to which this book might serve as prolegomena. Those who produce their own edition of even a short passage of a Shakespeare play, with their own modernized spelling and punctuation, emendations, added or altered stage directions, lineation, annotation, collation, and perhaps even introduction, are uniquely placed to engage with the complexities of the Shakespearean text and its editorial constructedness. There may be no better way of coming to a full understanding of how Shakespeare's texts as we read them today are always the result of modern collaborations.

Abbreviations

Since this is a book about Shakespeare's modern editors, I frequently refer to them and their editions in the course of the preceding pages. For ease of reference, I use the abbreviations listed below for complete works or series of single-play editions. Throughout my text, I provide full bibliographical information about individual volumes only to the extent that it seems of importance. Full information about them can be found in the 'Chronological Appendix' to Andrew Murphy's *Shakespeare in Print: A History and Chronology of Shakespeare Publishing* (Cambridge: Cambridge University Press, 2003). I mostly quote from editions which I identify in the text, but when I do not, the text and act-scene-and-line references are from David Bevington's *Complete Works*, 5th ed.

Arden 3	David Scott Kastan, Richard Proudfoot, and Ann Thompson, gen. eds, *The Arden Shakespeare* (London: Routledge; Walton-on-Thames: Thomas Nelson; London: Thomson Learning, 1995–)
Arden 2	Una Ellis-Fermor, Harold F. Brooks, Harold Jenkins, Brian Morris, gen. eds, *The Arden Shakespeare* (London: Methuen, 1951–82)
Arden 1	W. J. Craig and R. H. Case, gen. eds, *The Arden Shakespeare* (London: Methuen, 1899–1931)

Arden *Complete Works*	D. S. Kastan, Richard Proudfoot, and Ann Thompson, gen. eds, *The Arden Shakespeare Complete Works* (Walton-on-Thames: Thomas Nelson, 1998)
Bate and Rasmussen	Jonathan Bate and Eric Rasmussen, eds, *William Shakespeare: The Complete Works* (Basingstoke: Palgrave Macmillan, 2007)
Bevington	David Bevington, ed., *The Complete Works of Shakespeare*, 5th ed. (New York: Longman, 2003)
Bevington, updated 4th ed.	David Bevington, ed., *The Complete Works of Shakespeare*, updated 4th ed. (New York: Longman, 1997)
Craig/Bevington	Hardin Craig and David Bevington, eds, *The Complete Works of Shakespeare* (Glenview, IL: Scott, Foresman & Co., 1973)
Folger	Barbara A. Mowat and Paul Werstine, eds, *Folger Shakespeare Library* (New York: Washington Square, 1992–)
Norton	Stephen Greenblatt, gen. ed., *The Norton Shakespeare: Based on the Oxford Edition* (New York: Norton, 1997)
New Cambridge	Philip Brockbank, Brian Gibbons, A. R. Braunmuller, Robin Hood, gen. eds, *The New Cambridge Shakespeare* (Cambridge: Cambridge University Press, 1984–) (page references are to

	the original rather than to the recent, updated editions)
New Penguin	T. J. B. Spencer, gen. ed., Stanley Wells, assoc. ed., *The New Penguin Shakespeare* (Harmondsworth: Penguin, 1967–2005)
Oxford	Stanley Wells, gen. ed., *The Oxford Shakespeare* (Oxford: Clarendon, 1982–)
Oxford *Complete Works*	Stanley Wells and Gary Taylor, gen. eds, *The Oxford Shakespeare: The Complete Works*, 2nd ed. (Oxford: Oxford University Press, 2005, first publ. 1986)
Riverside	G. Blakemore Evans, with J. J. M. Tobin, gen. eds, *The Riverside Shakespeare*, 2nd ed. (Boston: Houghton Mifflin, 1997; 1st ed. 1974)

Notes

1 For the first three forms of collaboration, see, in particular, Brian Vickers, *Shakespeare, Co-Author: A Historical Study of Five Collaborative Plays* (Oxford: Oxford University Press, 2002); Tiffany Stern, *Making Shakespeare: From Page to Stage* (London: Routledge, 2004); and Charlton Hinman, *The Printing and Proof-reading of the First Folio of Shakespeare*, 2 vols (Oxford: Clarendon Press, 1963).

2 See Roslyn L. Knutson, *The Repertory of Shakespeare's Company, 1594–1613* (Fayetteville, Ark.: University of Arkansas Press, 1991).

3 Philip Gaskell, *From Writer to Reader: Studies in Editorial Method* (Oxford: Clarendon Press, 1978), p.15.

4 *King Richard II*, Arden 3, p.537.

5 R. A. Foakes, 'Shakespeare Editing and Textual Theory: A Rough Guide', *Huntington Library Quarterly*, 60 (1999), 425.

6 Margreta de Grazia and Peter Stallybrass, 'The Materiality of the Shakespearean Text', *Shakespeare Quarterly*, 44 (1993), 255.

7 De Grazia and Stallybrass, 'The Materiality of the Shakespearean Text', 255.

8 Michael Warren, 'Textual Problems, Editorial Assertions in Editions of Shakespeare', in *Textual Criticism and Literary Interpretation*, ed. Jerome McGann (Chicago: University of Chicago Press, 1985), p.27.

9 Warren, 'Textual Problems, Editorial Assertions in Editions of Shakespeare', p.34.

10 Randall McLeod, 'Un-Editing Shak-speare', *Sub-Stance*, 33–4 (1982), 38.

11 McLeod, 'Un-Editing Shak-speare', 40.

12 Warren, 'Textual Problems, Editorial Assertions in Editions of Shakespeare', p.33.

13 W. Speed Hill, 'Where We Are and How We Got Here: Editing after Post-Structuralism', *Shakespeare Studies*, 24 (1996), 40.

14 Warren, 'Textual Problems, Editorial Assertions in Editions of Shakespeare', p.35.

15 Stanley Wells, 'To Read a Play: The Problem of Editorial Intervention', in *Reading Plays: Interpretation and Reception*, eds Hanna Scolnicov and Peter Holland (Cambridge: Cambridge University Press, 1991), p.34.

16 Warren, 'Textual Problems, Editorial Assertions in Editions of Shakespeare', p.37.

17 McLeod, 'Un-Editing Shak-speare', 37.

18 T. H. Howard-Hill, 'The Dangers of Editing, or, the Death of the Editor', in *The Editorial Gaze: Mediating Texts in Literature and the Arts*, eds Paul Eggert and Margaret Sankey (New York: Garland Publishing, 1998), p.61.

19 De Grazia and Stallybrass, 'The Materiality of the Shakespearean Text', 282.

20 Peter L. Shillingsburg, 'Negotiating Conflicting Aims in Scholarly Editing: The Problem of Editorial Intentions', in *Problems of Editing*, ed. Christa Jansohn (Tübingen: Niemeyer, 1999), p.3.

21 Stephen Orgel, *The Authentic Shakespeare and Other Problems of the Early Modern Stage* (New York: Routledge, 2002), p.18.

22 References to early printed books are cited using the pagination markers then in use, namely the alphabetically ordered gathering of pages (E, for example), the page within the gathering, and the front or back of the page ('r' for recto, 'v' for verso).

23 David Scott Kastan, *Shakespeare after Theory* (New York: Routledge, 1999), p.68.

24 H. R. Woudhuysen, 'The Foundations of Shakespeare's Text', in *Proceedings of the British Academy: 2003 Lectures* (Oxford: Oxford University Press, 2004), p.99.

25 Brian Gibbons, series editor's preface, *The New Cambridge Shakespeare: The Early Quartos*, p.5.

26 Kastan, *Shakespeare after Theory*, p.69.

27 W. B. Worthen, *Print and the Poetics of Modern Drama* (Cambridge: Cambridge University Press, 2005), p.10.

28 Worthen, *Print and the Poetics of Modern Drama*, p.10.

29 Kastan, *Shakespeare after Theory*, p.69.

30 Leah Marcus, 'Shakespearean Editing and Why It Matters', *Literature Compass*, 2 (2005), SH 119, 2–3.

31 Leah Marcus, *Unediting the Renaissance: Shakespeare, Marlowe, Milton* (London and New York: Routledge, 1996), p.5.

32 David Bevington, 'Editing Renaissance Drama in Paperback', *Renaissance Drama*, 19 (1988), 136.

33 Bevington, 'Editing Renaissance Drama in Paperback', 134–5.

34 Suzanne Gossett, 'Editing Collaborative Drama', *Shakespeare Survey*, 59 (2006), 215.

35 See John F. Andrews, ed., *The Guild Shakespeare* (Garden City, NY: Doubleday Book & Music Clubs, Inc., 1989).

36 Riverside, p.67.

37 Stanley Wells, *Modernizing Shakespeare's Spelling*, with Gary Taylor, *Three Studies in the Text of 'Henry V'* (Oxford: Clarendon Press, 1979), p.5.

38 Bevington, 'Editing Renaissance Drama in Paperback', 137.

39 Riverside, p.68.

40 Here and below, I refer to the through-line numbering (TLN) adopted in Charlton Hinman, ed., *The First Folio of Shakespeare: The Norton Facsimile*, 2nd ed. (New York: Norton, 1996; 1st ed. 1968).

41 David Bevington, 'Modern Spelling: The Hard Choices', in *Textual Performances*, eds Erne and Kidnie, p.151.

42 See Stanley Wells, *Re-Editing Shakespeare for the Modern Reader* (Oxford: Clarendon Press, 1984), p.11.

43 Gaskell, *From Writer to Reader*, p.8.

44 De Grazia and Stallybrass, 'The Materiality of the Shakespearean Text', 266.

45 Warren, 'Textual Problems, Editorial Assertions in Editions of Shakespeare', 33.

46 De Grazia and Stallybrass, 'The Materiality of the Shakespearean Text', 263.

47 De Grazia and Stallybrass, 'The Materiality of the Shakespearean Text', 263.

48 See Percy Simpson, *Shakespearian Punctuation* (Oxford: Clarendon Press, 1911).

49 Wells, *Modernizing Shakespeare's Spelling*, p.31.

50 W. Speed Hill, 'Where are the Bibliographers of Yesteryear?', *Editio*, 14 (1999), 104.

51 Michael Warren, 'Repunctuation as Interpretation in Editions of Shakespeare', *English Literary Renaissance*, 7 (1977), 157.

52 Anthony Graham-White, *Punctuation and Its Dramatic Value in Shakespearean Drama* (Newark: University of Delaware Press, 1995), p.134.

53 Bevington, 'Editing Renaissance Drama in Paperback', 136.

54 Bevington, 'Editing Renaissance Drama in Paperback', 134–5.

55 John Dover Wilson, ed., *Hamlet*, The New Shakespeare (Cambridge: Cambridge University Press, 1934), p.76.

56 Gary Taylor, 'Inventing Shakespeare', *Shakespeare Jahrbuch West*, 122 (1986), 26.

57 Wells, *Re-Editing Shakespeare for the Modern Reader*, pp.33–56.

58 Hyder E. Rollins, ed. *The Sonnets*, A New Variorum Edition of

Shakespeare, 2 vols (Philadelphia: J. B. Lippincott, 1944), vol.1, pp.358–9.

59 Helen Vendler, *The Art of Shakespeare's Sonnets* (Cambridge, MA: Harvard University Press, 1997), pp.610–16.

60 See Michael Warren, 'The Perception of Error: the Editing and the Performance of the Opening of *Coriolanus*', in *Textual Performances*, eds Erne and Kidnie, pp.127–42.

61 Duncan Salkeld, 'Falstaff's Nose', *Notes and Queries*, 51 (2004), 284–5.

62 W. W. Greg, *Principles of Emendation*, Annual Shakespeare Lecture of the British Academy (London: Humphrey Milford, 1928), p.3.

63 Fredson Bowers, *On Editing Shakespeare* (Charlottesville: University of Virginia Press, 1966), p.167.

64 Arthur Sherbo, ed., *Johnson on Shakespeare*, *The Yale Edition of the Works of Samuel Johnson*, vol.7 (New Haven: Yale University Press, 1968), p.108.

65 Taylor, 'Inventing Shakespeare', 32.

66 Brian Vickers, 'Are All of Them by Shakespeare?', *The Times Literary Supplement*, August 11, 2006, p.11. See also David Bevington's complaint about the edition's 'textual adventurism' (Bevington, 'Determining the Indeterminate: The Oxford Shakespeare', *Shakespeare Quarterly*, 38 (1987), 503).

67 See Jeanne Addison Roberts, '"Wife" or "Wise" – *The Tempest*, l. 1786', *Studies in Bibliography*, 31 (1978), 203–8.

68 Stephen Orgel, 'Prospero's Wife', *Representations*, 8 (1984), 13.

69 *The Tempest*, Arden 3, p.137.

70 Stanley Wells and Gary Taylor, with John Jowett and William Montgomery, *William Shakespeare: A Textual Companion* (Oxford: Clarendon Press, 1987), p.616.

71 See Ronald A. Tumelson II, 'Ferdinand's Wife and Prospero's Wife', *Shakespeare Survey*, 59 (2006), 79–90.

72 *Macbeth*, Arden 2, p.xiii.

73 *Macbeth*, Arden 2, pp.xiii–xiv.

74 Andrew Gurr, 'Editing Stefano's Book', *Shakespeare Survey*, 59 (2006), 98.

75 Fredson Bowers, 'Establishing Shakespeare's Text: Notes on Short Lines and the Problem of Verse Division', *Studies in Bibliography*, 33 (1980), 75.

76 See Paul Bertram, *White Spaces in Shakespeare: The Development of the Modern Text* (Cleveland, Ohio: Bellflower Press, 1980).

77 Paul Werstine, 'Line Division in Shakespeare's Dramatic Verse: An Editorial Problem', *Analytical and Enumerative Bibliography*, 8 (1984), 118.

78 Bevington, updated 4th ed., viii.

79 Bevington, 'Editing Renaissance Drama in Paperback', 145.

80 Orgel, *The Authentic Shakespeare and Other Problems of the Early Modern Stage*, p.38.

81 Orgel, *The Authentic Shakespeare and Other Problems of the Early Modern Stage*, pp.38–9.

82 See Patricia Parker, 'Altering the Letter of *Twelfth Night*: "Some Are Born Great" and the Missing Signature', *Shakespeare Survey*, 59 (2006), 49–62.

83 See Alex Preminger and T. V. F. Brogan, eds, *The New Princeton Encyclopedia of Poetry and Poetics* (Princeton: Princeton University Press, 1993).

84 Wilfred T. Jewkes, *Act Division in Elizabethan and Jacobean Plays 1583–1616* (Hamden, Conn.: Shoe String Press, 1958), pp.97–8.

85 See R. A. Foakes, ed., *Henslowe's Diary*, 2nd ed. (Cambridge: Cambridge University Press, 2002).

86 See Emrys Jones, *Scenic Form in Shakespeare* (Oxford: Clarendon Press, 1971), p.68.

87 *Hamlet*, Arden 3, pp.544–5.

88 Bevington, 'Editing Renaissance Drama in Paperback', 145.

89 Wells et al., *William Shakespeare: A Textual Companion*, p.402.

90 *Hamlet*, Arden 3, pp.551–2.

91 See *Romeo and Juliet*, Oxford, p.316.

92 *Romeo and Juliet*, New Cambridge, p.169.

93 Harley Granville-Barker, *Prefaces to Shakespeare*, 4 vols (London: Batsford, 1963), vol.4, pp.62–3.

94 William A. Ringler, Jr, 'The Number of Actors in Shakespeare's Early Plays', in *The Seventeenth-Century Stage: A Collection of Critical Essays*, ed. G. E. Bentley (Chicago: University of Chicago Press, 1968), p.114.

95 George Walton Williams, 'Scene Individable: The Battle of Birnam Wood', *The Shakespeare Newsletter*, 55.2 (Summer 2005), 33, 36.

96 Williams, 'Scene Individable: The Battle of Birnam Wood', 36.

97 See Lukas Erne, 'Shakespeare for Readers', in *Alternative Shakespeares 3*, ed. Diana Henderson (London: Routledge, 2007)., pp.78–94.

98 Emrys Jones, *The Origins of Shakespeare* (Oxford: Clarendon Press, 1977), pp.27–8.

99 See De Grazia and Stallybrass, 'The Materiality of the Shakespearean Text', 267.

100 See L. C. Knights, 'How Many Children Had Lady Macbeth?' (1933), repr. in Knights, *Explorations: Essays in Criticism Mainly on the Literature of the Seventeenth Century* (New York: George W. Stewart, 1946), pp.1–39.

101 Cloud, Random (Randall McLeod), '"The very names of the Persons": Editing and the Invention of Dramatick Character', *Staging the Renaissance: Reinterpretations of Elizabethan and Jacobean Drama*, eds David Scott Kastan and Peter Stallybrass (London: Routledge, 1991), p.95; Laurie E. Maguire, 'Feminist Editing and the Body of the Text', in *A Feminist Companion to Shakespeare*, ed. Dympna Callaghan (Oxford: Blackwell, 2000), p.73.

102 David Crystal and Ben Crystal, *Shakespeare's Words: A Glossary and Language Companion* (London: Penguin Books, 2002), p.513.

103 See Audrey Stanley, 'What Is Hymen?', *On Stage Studies*, 4 (1980), 70–83.

104 See David A. Griffin, 'Deus ex Machina in *As You Like It*', *American Notes and Queries*, 9 (1970), 23–4.

105 *As You Like It*, Arden 2, p.126.

106 See Timothy Billings, *Glossing Shakespeare: Reading the Plays from the Bottom of the Page* (Basingstoke: Palgrave, forthcoming).

107 Samuel Johnson, 'Preface to Shakespeare, 1765', in *Johnson on Shakespeare*, ed. Arthur Sherbo, *The Yale Edition of the Works of Samuel Johnson*, vol.VII (New Haven: Yale University Press, 1968), p.111.

108 John Pitcher, 'Why Editors Should Write More Notes', *Shakespeare Studies*, 24 (1996), 58, 60.

109 Helen Wilcox, 'The Character of a Footnote . . . Or, Annotation Revisited', in *In Arden: Editing Shakespeare*, eds Ann Thompson and Gordon McMullan (London: Thompson Learning, 2003), p.205.

110 Wilcox, 'The Character of a Footnote . . . Or, Annotation Revisited', p.205.

111 Maguire, 'Feminist Editing and the Body of the Text', p.71.

112 Maguire, 'Feminist Editing and the Body of the Text', p.65.

113 See Michael Cordner, 'Annotation and Performance in Shakespeare', *Essays in Criticism*, 46 (1996), 289–301.

114 Cordner, 'Annotation and Performance in Shakespeare', 291.

115 Wilcox, 'The Character of a Footnote . . . Or, Annotation Revisited', pp.197–9.

116 Cordner, 'Annotation and Performance in Shakespeare', 293.

117 G. K. Hunter, 'The Social Function of Annotation', in *In Arden*, eds Thompson and McMullan, p.177.

Notes 119

118 Eric Rasmussen, 'Richly Noted: A Case for Collation Inflation' in *In Arden*, eds Thompson and McMullan, p.211.

119 Robert Kean Turner and Virginia Westling Haas, eds, *The Winter's Tale*, The New Variorum Edition of Shakespeare (New York: Modern Language Association of America, 2005), p.ix.

120 Rasmussen, 'Richly Noted: A Case for Collation Inflation', p.216.

121 Sonia Massai, *Shakespeare and the Rise of the Editor* (Cambridge: Cambridge University Press, 2007).

122 John Edwards, 'Absent Footnotes', *The Times Literary Supplement*, June 24, 2005, p.17.

123 Stanley Wells, 'On Being a General Editor', *Shakespeare Survey*, 59 (2006), 48.

124 *Love's Labour's Lost*, Arden 3, p.111.

125 E. K. Chambers, *William Shakespeare: A Study of Facts and Problems*, 2 vols (Oxford: Clarendon Press, 1930), vol.1, pp.539–42.

126 See MacDonald P. Jackson, 'Shakespeare and the Quarrel Scene in *Arden of Faversham*', *Shakespeare Quarterly*, 57 (2006), 249–93.

127 Wells et al., *William Shakespeare: A Textual Companion*, p.119.

128 Anthony Hammond, 'Encounters of the Third Kind in Stage-Directions in Elizabethan and Jacobean Drama', *Studies in Philology*, 89 (1992), 81.

129 Alan C. Dessen, *Recovering Shakespeare's Theatrical Vocabulary* (Cambridge: Cambridge University Press, 1995), p.6.

130 M. J. Kidnie, 'The Staging of Shakespeare's Drama in Print Editions', in *Textual Performances*, eds Erne and Kidnie, p.160.

131 Wells, *Re-Editing Shakespeare for the Modern Reader*, p.63.

132 Wells, *Re-Editing Shakespeare for the Modern Reader*, p.76.

133 See Wells, *Re-Editing Shakespeare for the Modern Reader*, pp.72–3.

134 Wells et al., *William Shakespeare: A Textual Companion*, p.601.

135 See Wells, *Re-Editing Shakespeare for the Modern Reader*, p.74.

136 New Cambridge, *The First Quarto of Romeo and Juliet*, pp.159–65.

137 Marvin Rosenberg, *The Masks of 'Hamlet'* (Newark: University of Delaware Press, 1992), p.924.

138 Dieter Mehl, 'Hamlet's Last Moments: A Note on John Russell Brown', *Connotations*, 2 (1992), 183.

139 Rosenberg, *The Masks of 'Hamlet'*, p.385.

140 George Walton Williams, 'To Edit? To Direct? Ay, There's the Rub', in *In Arden*, eds Thompson and McMullan, pp.112–13.

141 Williams, 'To Edit? To Direct? Ay, There's the Rub', p.119.

142 Williams, 'To Edit? To Direct? Ay, There's the Rub', p.121.

143 R. A. Foakes, 'Raw Flesh/Lion's Flesh: A Cautionary Note on Stage Directions', in *In Arden*, eds Thompson and McMullan, p.136.

144 A. R. Braunmuller, 'On Not Looking Back: Sight and Sound and Text', in *From Performance to Print*, eds Holland and Orgel, p.148.

145 *1 Henry IV*, Arden 3, p.129.

146 M. J. Kidnie, 'Text, Performance, and the Editors: Staging Shakespeare's Drama', *Shakespeare Quarterly*, 51 (2000), 472.

147 John D. Cox, 'Open Stage, Open Page? Editing Stage Directions in Early Dramatic Texts', in *Textual Performances*, eds Erne and Kidnie, p.178.

148 Braunmuller, 'On Not Looking Back: Sight and Sound and Text', p.146.

149 Wells, *Re-Editing Shakespeare for the Modern Reader*, p.68.

150 Wells, 'To Read a Play: The Problem of Editorial Intervention', p.46.

151 Wells, 'To Read a Play: The Problem of Editorial Intervention', p.46.

152 Braunmuller, 'On Not Looking Back: Sight and Sound and Text', p.148.

153 Kidnie, 'Text, Performance, and the Editors: Staging Shakespeare's Drama', 469.

154 Kidnie, 'The Staging of Shakespeare's Drama in Print Editions', p.163.

155 Kidnie, 'The Staging of Shakespeare's Drama in Print Editions', p.164.

156 Kidnie, 'The Staging of Shakespeare's Drama in Print Editions', p.172.

157 See Walter J. Ong, S.J., 'The Writer's Audience Is Always a Fiction', *PMLA*, 90 (1975), 9–21.

158 Wells, *Re-Editing Shakespeare for the Modern Reader*, p.69.

159 Wells, *Re-Editing Shakespeare for the Modern Reader*, pp.68, 70.

160 Kidnie, 'Text, Performance, and the Editors: Staging Shakespeare's Drama', 465–6.

161 Wells, *Re-Editing Shakespeare for the Modern Reader*, p.69.

162 Kidnie, 'Text, Performance, and the Editors: Staging Shakespeare's Drama', 459.

163 Stephen Orgel, 'The Book of the Play', in *From Performance to Print*, eds Holland and Orgel, p.44.

164 Alan C. Dessen and Leslie Thomson, *A Dictionary of Stage Directions in English Drama, 1580–1642* (Cambridge: Cambridge University Press, 1999), p.251.

165 Dessen and Thomson, *A Dictionary of Stage Directions in English Drama, 1580–1642*, p.242.

166 Dessen and Thomson, *A Dictionary of Stage Directions in English Drama, 1580–1642*, p.58.

167 Dessen and Thomson, *A Dictionary of Stage Directions in English Drama, 1580–1642*, p.90.

168 Wells, *Re-Editing Shakespeare for the Modern Reader*, p.69.

169 Kidnie, 'The Staging of Shakespeare's Drama in Print Editions', p.161.

170 Orgel, 'The Book of the Play', 28.

171 R. A. Foakes, *Illustrations of the English Stage 1580–1642* (London: Scolar Press, 1985), p.105.

172 Foakes, *Illustrations of the English Stage 1580–1642*, pp.114–15.

173 Orgel, 'The Book of the Play', 48.

174 Foakes, ed. *King Lear*, Arden 3, p.113.

175 See Michael Warren, 'Quarto and Folio *King Lear* and the Interpretation of Albany and Edgar', in *Shakespeare: Pattern of Excelling Nature*, eds David Bevington and Jay L. Halio (Newark: University of Delaware Press, 1978), pp.95–107.

176 See Gary Taylor, 'The War in *King Lear*', *Shakespeare Survey*, 33 (1980), 27–34; Steven Urkowitz, *Shakespeare's Revision of 'King Lear'* (Princeton: Princeton University Press, 1980).

177 See Gary Taylor and Michael Warren, eds, *The Division of the Kingdoms* (Oxford: Clarendon Press, 1983).

178 Urkowitz, *Shakespeare's Revision of 'King Lear'*, p.149.

179 See Richard Knowles, 'Two *Lear*s? By Shakespeare?', in *Lear from Study to Stage: Essays in Criticism*, eds James Ogden and Arthur H. Scouten (Madison: Fairleigh Dickinson University Press, 1997), pp.57–78.

180 René Weis, ed., *'King Lear': A Parallel Text Edition* (London: Longman, 1993), p.34.

181 Vickers, 'Are All of Them by Shakespeare?', p.12.

182 Vickers, 'Are All of Them by Shakespeare?', p.12.

183 *King Lear*, Arden 3, pp.118–19.

184 Urkowitz, *Shakespeare's Revision of 'King Lear'*, pp.16–17.

185 See Robert Clare, '"Who is it that can tell me who I am?": The Theory of Authorial Revision between the Quarto and Folio Texts of *King Lear*', *The Library*, 6th series 17 (1995), 34–59.

186 See Roger Warren, 'The Folio Omission of the Mock Trial: Motives and Consequences', in *The Division of the Kingdoms*,

eds Gary Taylor and Michael Warren (Oxford: Clarendon Press, 1983), pp.45–57.

187 See William C. Carroll, 'New Plays vs. Old Readings: *The Division of the Kingdoms* and Folio Deletions in *King Lear*', *Studies in Philology*, 85 (1988), 225–44.

188 Paul Werstine, review of E. A. J. Honigmann, *The Texts of 'Othello' and Shakespearian Revision*, *Shakespeare Quarterly*, 51 (2000), 241.

189 See J. K. Walton, 'Lear's Last Speech', *Shakespeare Survey*, 13 (1960), 11–19; Derek Peat, '"And that's true too": *King Lear* and the Tension of Uncertainty', *Shakespeare Survey*, 33 (1980), 43–53; Ian Kirby, 'The Passing of King Lear', *Shakespeare Survey*, 41 (1989), 145–57.

190 A. C. Bradley, *Shakespearean Tragedy: Lectures on 'Hamlet', 'Othello', 'King Lear', 'Macbeth'* (London: Macmillan, 1904), p.291.

191 See, for instance, William Empson, *The Structure of Complex Words* (London: Chatto & Windus, 1951), p.152; G. Wilson Knight, *The Wheel of Fire* (Oxford: Oxford University Press, 1930), p.176; *King Lear*, Arden 2, p.lix.

192 Stephen J. Greenblatt, *Learning to Curse: Essays in Early Modern Culture* (New York: Routledge, 1990), p.98.

193 Frank Kermode, *Shakespeare's Language* (Harmondsworth: Penguin Press, 2000), p.199.

194 Riverside, p.1344.

195 *King Lear*, Folger, p.lxi.

196 *King Lear*, Folger, p.lxii.

197 In the introduction to his New Cambridge Shakespeare edition of *The Tragedy of King Lear*, Halio (pp.82–9) offers sample passages of a parallel-text edition in which all substantive differences are typographically highlighted for easier visibility, yet another editorial solution to the problem of the texts of *King Lear*.

198 *Hamlet*, Arden 2, p.75.

199 Stanley Wells and Gary Taylor, 'The Oxford Shakespeare Reviewed', *Analytical and Enumerative Bibliography*, 4 (1990), 16.

200 Murphy, *Shakespeare in Print*, 279–386.

201 Kidnie, 'Staging Shakespeare's Drama in Print Editions', pp.164–5.

202 John Lavagnino, 'Two Varieties of Digital Commentary', in *Textual Performances*, eds Erne and Kidnie, p.194.

203 Lavagnino, 'Two Varieties of Digital Commentary', pp.198–200.

Index

abridgement 2
act division 34–36, *see also* scene division
Alexander, Peter 78
All's Well that Ends Well 39, 57, 58
annotation 40, 46–48, 51–52, 71, 72, 74, 75, 76, 105
Antony and Cleopatra 18, 35, 54, 57, 58, 81, 91
apparatus, editorial 43–58, *see also* annotation, appendix, collation, dramatis personae list, introduction, title
appendix 54
Arden Shakespeare 13, 43, 47, 50, 52, 53
   Arden1 47, 78
   Arden2 20, 21, 24, 26, 30, 34, 39, 40, 43, 45, 50, 51, 52, 53, 54, 62, 65, 67, 70, 73, 78, 100
   Arden3 18, 20, 22, 25, 36, 37, 40, 41, 45, 46, 47, 51, 52, 53, 54, 55, 56, 78, 97–98, 101
Arden *Complete Works* 57
Arden of Faversham 2, 57
As You Like It 22, 45–46, 52, 53
Ariosto, Ludovico
   Orlando Furioso 3
authorship 1–2, *see also* collaboration

Baldwin, T. S. 35
Bantam Shakespeare 36, 51, 54
Bate, Jonathan and Eric Rasmussen, *Complete Works* 55, 56, 57, 76, 97
Beaumont, Francis, and John Fletcher
   A King and No King 84
   The Maid's Tragedy 84
Becket, Samuel 10
Berni, Francesco 33
Bertram, Paul 27, 101
Best, Michael 104
Bevington, David 10, 14, 15, 28, 36, 56, 97
Bevington, *Complete Works* 13–14, 15, 16, 19, 20, 21, 22, 25, 29, 30, 34, 41, 45, 56, 57, 62, 65, 78, 96–97
Bible, The 46
blank verse, *see* verse
Blayney, Peter W. M. 24
Booth, Stephen 18
Bowers, Fredson 23, 55
Bradley, A. C. 44, 90
Braunmuller, A. R. 71, 72, 74
Burbage, Richard 53–54, 69

canon 56–57
Capell, Edward 27
Cardenio 56

Index

Chambers, E. K. 56
character, *see* names of characters, dramatis personae list
co-authorship, *see* collaboration
collaboration 1–4
collation 48–51
commentary, *see* annotation
complete works 56–58
conflation 88, *see also King Lear*
1 Contention of the Two Famous Houses of York and Lancaster 55–56
Cordner, Michael 48
Coriolanus 54, 81, 82
Coward, Noël 52
Cox, John 72, 76
Craig/Bevington, *Complete Works* 41, 45, 78
Crystal, David and Ben 45
Cymbeline 39, 57, 82, 96

D'Avenant, William 54
De Grazia, Margreta 5
Dessen, Alan C. 60, 82
digital editions, *see* electronic editions
Donne, John 26, 69
Dowden, Edward 70, 75
dramatis personae list 43–46
Dusinberre, Juliet 46

Edward III 2, 56, 101
Edwards, Philip 100
electronic editions 101, 104–5
emendation 20–25
Evans, G. Blakemore 37, 97

facsimiles 6–7, 99
film 64, 104
First Folio 1, 3, 7, 15, 17, 19–20, 22, 23, 24, 25, 26, 27, 28, 29, 35, 36, 38, 39, 40, 41, 43, 44, 49, 50, 55, 56, 57, 61, 63, 68, 81, 82, 88–101
Fletcher, John 2, 56, *see also* Beaumont, *Cardenio*
Foakes, R. A. 5, 71, 76, 97, 102
Folger Shakespeare 24, 29, 38, 45, 46, 51, 70, 75, 98, 100
folios 7, 16, 18, 29, 44, 49, 51, 54–55, 92
footnotes, *see* annotation

Garrick, David 54
gender 66–67
Gibbons, Brian 8
Gielgud, John 54
Gossett, Suzanne 13
Granville-Barker, Harley 37
Greenblatt, Stephen 96
Greg, W. W. 23, 36
Guild Shakespeare, The 13

Halio, J. L. 97, 102
Hamlet 2, 8, 13, 19–20, 33, 35–36, 40, 47, 50, 52, 68–71, 81, 82, 100–102, 103, 104
Hammond, Anthony 60
Harington, Sir John 3
1 Henry IV 70
2 Henry IV 39, 43, 100, 104
Henry V 22, 35, 44, 48, 49, 55, 77, 82, 103, 104
1 Henry VI 2, 57
2 Henry VI 2, 35, 55, 57, 81, 82
3 Henry VI 2, 35, 56, 57, 81
Henry VIII 2, 41, 53, 54, 55, 81
Henslowe, Philip 35
Hibbard, G. R. 68–69, 100
Holinshed, Raphael 17
Hosley, Richard 83
Hunter, G. K. 48
hypertext, *see* electronic editions

Index

illustrations, *see* woodcut
imperialism 9
index 53
introduction 52–54, 103–4

Jenkins, Harold 100
Jones, Emrys 36
Johnson, Samuel 4, 23, 36, 46
Jonson, Ben 28, 44
Julius Caesar 82

Kastan, David Scott 71
Kermode, Frank 24
Kidnie, M. J. 60–61, 71–72, 75–76, 79–80, 83
King John 58, 81, 82
King Lear 4, 5, 10–11, 29, 37, 52, 53, 58, 59, 87–102, 103, 104
  authorial revision 88–89
  conflation 96–100
  Lear's death 90–94, 95
  speech assignment 88, 94
  variant early texts 87–100
  versioning 96–100
Kittredge, G. L. 50
Kliman, Bernice W. 101, 104
Knights, L. C. 44
Knowles, Richard 49
Kyd, Thomas
  The Spanish Tragedy 84

Latham, Agnes 46
Lavagnino, John 105
layout 31–33, 51–52, 76, 103
Levenson, Jill 30, 74, 75
lineation 25–29, *see also* long lines, shared lines, short lines
long lines, 25, 92
Love's Labour's Lost 54–55, 58
Love's Labour's Won 58

Macbeth 2, 13, 15, 17, 25–27, 28–29, 38–39, 40–41, 44, 45, 50, 53, 54, 58, 80
Macready, William Charles 54, 87
Maguire, Laurie 47
Marcus, Leah 9–10
Massai, Sonia 51
McKerrow, Ronald 37
McLeod, Randall 6
Measure for Measure 43, 78, 79
Mehl, Dieter 69
The Merchant of Venice 15, 39, 53, 81
meter 21, 25–31
Middleton, Thomas 2, *see also Timon of Athens*
A Midsummer Night's Dream 39, 45, 57–58, 77–78
Milton, John 24
  'On the New Forcers of Conscience Under the Long Parliament' 33
Moxon, Joseph
  Mechanick Exercises on the Whole Art of Printing 3
Much Ado About Nothing 20–21
Muir, Kenneth 26
multiple-text plays 19–20, 66–69, 87–105
Murphy, Andrew 49

names of characters 39–41
Neill, Michael 54
New Cambridge Shakespeare 13, 21, 22, 24, 29, 38, 40, 43, 44, 45, 48, 49, 50, 51, 53, 54, 55, 56, 65, 67, 75, 78, 97, 100
New Penguin Shakespeare 19, 21, 29, 30, 38, 48, 51, 55
New Variorum Shakespeare 49
Norton Shakespeare 78, 96
No Sweat Shakespeare 13
notes, *see* annotation

Ong, Walter 76
Orgel, Stephen 7, 24, 30, 80, 84
Othello 35, 43, 45, 81, 96, 100, 103, 104
Oxford *Complete Works* 14, 15, 21, 23, 25, 29, 30, 31, 36, 38, 40, 41, 45, 46, 50, 51–52, 55, 56, 57, 62, 65, 66, 70, 73, 74, 78, 79, 95–96, 100
Oxford Shakespeare 13, 19, 21, 22, 24, 29, 30, 38, 43, 45, 50, 51, 53, 54, 55, 65, 68, 74, 97, 100

paper 7
parallel-text edition 99, 101, 104
paratext, *see* apparatus
Parker, Patricia 31
Peele, George 1
performance 2, 6, 8, 53–54, 60
Pericles 1, 2, 23, 53, 56, 58, 82
Pinter, Harold 10
Pitcher, John 46
Pope, Alexander 21, 26, 78
prose 29–31
Prynne, William
    Histrio-mastix 7
punctuation 3, 17–18
    modernization of 17–20

Quiller-Couch, Arthur 77

Rasmussen, Eric 50 *see also* Bate, Jonathan
relineation, *see* lineation
revision, authorial 2, 88–89
rhyme 33–34
Richard II 3, 41, 52, 57, 58, 77, 78, 81
Richard III 79
Riverside Shakespeare 13, 14, 15, 17, 19, 20, 21, 29, 30, 34, 41, 44, 46, 56, 57, 70, 73, 78, 96, 97

Roberts, Jeanne Addison 24–25
Romeo and Juliet 21, 29–34, 35, 36–38, 44, 45, 51, 54, 57, 58, 64–67, 73–75, 103, 104
Rowe, Nicholas 35, 40

Salkeld, Duncan 23
scene division 34–39, *see also* act division
sexism 9
shared lines 27, 29
short lines 25, 28, 92
Sir Thomas More 2, 56, 101
Sonnets, The 18, 21
sonnet form 31–34
speech prefix 39–41
spelling 3, 6
    modernization of 13–17
Spenser, Edmund 15
stage directions 40, 59–85
    entrances 62–66, 77–78
    implied stage directions 59, 61–62, 69–70
    indications of locality 78
    literary stage directions 77–84
    theatrical stage directions 77–84
Stallybrass, Peter 5
Staunton, Howard 50
Steevens, George 27

Taming of the Shrew, The 53, 81
Tate, Nahum 87
Taylor, Gary 20, 23, 96
Taylor, Neil 36, 101
Tempest, The 9, 16–17, 24, 35, 43, 46, 82
text 13–42, *see also* emendation, meter, layout, lineation, long lines, multiple-text plays, prose, punctuation, rhyme, short lines, shared lines, spelling, verse

Theobald, Lewis 17, 22, 49, 63, 75, 88
  Double Falsehood 56
Thompson, Ann 36, 101
Thomson, Leslie 82–83
Timon of Athens 1, 35, 39, 43, 58, 79, 82, 96
title 54–56
Titus Andronicus 1, 35, 53, 57
Tronch-Pérez, Jesús 101
True Tragedy of Richard Duke of York, The 55–56
Troilus and Cressida 35, 54, 57, 79, 100, 104
Twelfth Night 31
Two Gentlemen of Verona, The 43, 44
Two Noble Kinsmen, The 2, 56, 57

'unediting' 5–10

Vendler, Helen 22
verse 25–31, 92

versioning, *see King Lear*

Warren, Michael 6, 99
Weis, René 99, 102
Wells, Stanley 14, 54, 73, 76, 78–79, 80, 83, 96, 97
Werstine, Paul 28, 49
Whole Contention between the Two Famous Houses, Lancaster and York, The 56
Wilkins, George 2
  The Painfull Adventures of Pericles Prince of Tyre 23
Williams, George Walton 38–39, 70–73, 76
Wilson, John Dover 20, 77–78, 83
Winter's Tale, The 43, 49, 56, 59, 61–53, 78, 96
woodcut illustrations 84
Worthen, W. B. 8
Woudhuysen, Henry 54